STO
OF THE CIA

INCLUDING THE LATEST SECRET MISSION

...AND OF THE US ARMY AND EUROPE

- WITH DOG AND SPORTS TALES THROWN IN -

A.V. WITTNER

Author email: avw_eur@yahoo.com

Design and formatting by Candace Nikiforou
Desktop Publishing Annapolis, Maryland

2009 Edition Included Herein as Part II
Front Cover Photograph - a kitten, a Great Dane
and a friendship that had to be seen to be believed

Many Color Photographs Included

ISBN-13: 978-0692873700
(Harbridge Hall - London)

ISBN-10: 0692873708

Distribution Through Amazon CreateSpace

Harbridge Hall
- London -

Author's Use of Images in Part I

I spent some 40 years in national security work, and there are none better nor more devoted than those at the various intelligence agencies. They are rarely seen and even more rarely thanked. I do thank them...again.

Yet Part I of this book is for the most part of humor, and I felt a few classic intelligence clip art images would be fitting. On the web, I found literally thousands...many on so-called "free" sites. Certain of the images I purchased under license from Dreamstime. The MAD images I found on one such free site, yet I felt they should not be free to "use". This MAD imagery has become almost an American classic; I wanted to use more.

I searched the web for MAD and was stonewalled. I was told by machine MAD was "in hiatus" and was even given a non-working phone number in New York City. I contacted offices in NY, Washington, DC and Texas. I have email records of my search. And, as I say, there were innumerable alternatives. Still I decided to use a few MAD images. MAD...you were wonderful! I only hope you may come out of hiatus...whatever that means.

I remain ready to pay for MAD imagery, at the Dreamstime price, if asked. I alone bear responsibility for use in this book.

I hope anyone reading this book urges you to do more... MAD. We need you at this incredibly bizarre time in Washington.

AVW 3/18/2017

CONTENTS

INTRODUCTION

FOREWORD

INTRODUCTION

Along with tales of the CIA and Army, baseball, fishing, and a few others, this book contains a reprint of my 2009 *Three Dogs, Some Satire, A Girl and Europe*. The idea was to get it all under one cover. The earlier took almost three years to get done. I never had it edited; I write free form for the most part and the thought of paying an editor was ridiculous. I write mostly as I speak..punctuation never bothers me too much. Nor has this version been edited. Can you imagine a discussion about a comma?

I never thought to sell. Still, a clever screen or stage writer might do some magic with a selected well woven package of these stories. We'll see.

Some 30 or so short tales, including those of the CIA and the US Army, are told in this version, as well as the dog stories of the earlier version but updated with our Appenzell-Eltebuch mix...Lord Rockaway of Downton Abbey. His is the final tale in Part l.

I might mention one author for whom, as a storyteller, I judge there is no match. He was elegant. He was detailed but never bored. His language was too beautiful. He wrote of dogs...*Travels With Charley*..and of the human condition. Many such. He ought to be read by popularist governments... by despots...by ham-headed bigots everywhere. He was not afraid to carry a rifle in his wandering. But he was smart. His name was John Steinbeck.

Him I thank.

Here we go.

FOREWORD

With 365 copies of Part II, the first in the series sold, it was time to move on. I wondered...might a dog write a book?

The idea of a dog trying to make some sense of today's world came to me both accidentally and by design. I'd wanted to write about the fabulously nice and intelligent dog we'd adopted two years ago and I'd recently re-read a book called *The Spy Who* did something or other by a Brit whose name we all know. And since I'd already done a few Europe-based stories, and knew a little Europe, I thought perhaps a so wise and observant dog could do no worse than did I... than do we at the top of the food chain. We the supreme predator. We who have no excuse but idiocy.

How to do this, I thought? I'd no idea. So I just started writing...*The Dog who came in from the Cold*.

I hoped that wonderful Brit author, John le Carre, wouldn't sue me. He is a true artist, not simply a genre writer, and I hoped my choice of title would do no one harm. Dogs after all, smart ones like mine...His Honorary Lordship Sir Rockaway of Long Island and Downton Abbey...are always coming in from the cold. This one had to; we needed him. He us.

Well, Rocky thought, *this life is now just fine. I have my home, several beds, my new family, new dog friends, enough money, health ok for now. Still he mused..might I write?*

Surely there are more stories to be chronicled, this world is so screwed up. Might as well give it a shot. Maybe the spy service can use a dog on the wall...watching? Would anyone notice? Nah...no chance. How could a dog, disguised or not, possibly be blown? Might I help these so screwed up humans?

As Rocky thought about this...how to pull it off...a number of other quick vignettes popped into my mind. I'd started jotting them down some time back and then just kind of forgot. I'd been writing only for myself, of course, as do all great writers. But I was a bit tired of me.

We'll leave Lord Rockaway, for a moment, to his study of Smiley, and run through a few nonsense observations and a number of short stories. Many are Army, CIA or otherwise security related. All point up why dogs should rule. A few are serious.

Rocky did give up the writing idea. But you'll meet him soon.

PART I

Stories of the CIA,
of the US Army and
with Sports and
Assorted Tales Thrown In.
Plus One Dog.

Headlines
You'll Never See

Ivanka Starts Day Care Center

Obama to Debate Melania

Trump Bares Barbados Tax Return

Merkel Wins Swimsuit Competition

Mexico Pressured to Take Texas Back; Balks

Texas Makes Primary Education Mandatory
for Governor

French *Agree!*

Greece to Pay All Debt!

Israel Returns Land to Palestinians, with Apology

Boehner's Hair Mussed; Wants Job Back

Ohio Republican Earns College Degree

Sanders Denies Brooklyn Roots

Chinese Food Outlawed in Iowa

Iowa Outlawed in Senate

Migrants Welcomed in Yemen (Both)

Schengen Declared Dead; Italy asks "who?"

Hollande Removes "e" From Name

Brexit and Grexit Engaged to Marry

First - September 11, 2001

I was working in Arlington, Virginia, quite close to the Pentagon. It was about 10 in the morning, and all eyes were on the computer screens, showing the towers in New York City. For some reason I went down to my car and in crossing the street I could clearly see the column of smoke rising from the Pentagon about a quarter mile away.

I knew not, then, what it was, but decided to beat the crowd and get out of town. As I drove home I heard on the radio of the Pentagon aircraft. The whole thing was so surrealistic. Arriving back in Annapolis I dropped in at my favorite coffee shop...and there it was on TV...just as we all know and remember.

Not a big story, just how it happened to me. I grew up in New York City and many first responders from my old neighborhood soon would be casualties.

As for the Pentagon, I had worked for many years in and near the section hit by the aircraft.

  # The
Central Intelligence Agency

From 1971 up to our move to Annapolis in 1993 we lived in McLean, Virginia, a few miles from CIA headquarters in Langley. Yes, the CIA was off limits unless you had business there, but nothing like it is today since the murderous attack out front...and later of course 9/11. I'd been inside many times on routine business, and once on a big time job interview. Here are a few CIA stories, all true.

THE CIA WEDDING

Across the street from us in McLean lived a great, and very democratic in their politics, quite senior CIA family. The husband was quite large and imposing, not one to joke very much. Lighthearted he was not, but sharp as could be. They had two grown sons and a daughter, with one son a rabid socialist – yes believe all this – living with his lady friend and other leftists, all in New York City.

Rumor had it that, in opposition to the Vietnam war, a son or two had zipped off to Canada. This kind of politics is not exactly CIA now, in the 2000s. The CIA, of course, has become an instrument of policy far more openly than back then. The neighbor wife was a product of the British diplomatic service. She smoked an occasional cigar.

Anyhow, the NY city socialist son announced to his parents he would marry his even more socialist NY girlfriend, and the wedding was set for their backyard across from us. Good so far. A happy CIA wedding.

The dad reputedly had delivered the Cuban missile photos to the desk of President Kennedy. He was later chief, again by rumor leaking out, of the National Photographic Intelligence Center, or whatever it was called in the 1960s. Pretty high up intelligence stuff in the cold war. Bear in mind the scary threat of nuclear weapons and how close we came to nuclear war during those years.

Ok, we all show up in their backyard. The family plus every imaginable senior CIA officer, including one who later became the CIA director, the top dog. All spread about in a beautiful half circle of intelligence. I was standing next to another neighbor, a guy who was then actively covert in Europe. So...CIA very top level staff all gathered

at a wedding...a socialist wedding. Yes, actively covert...
everyone knew.

And what is the socialist choice-for-reverend
preaching? Catch this now...he is outspokenly advocating the
forcible overthrow of the US government. That was a little
beyond socialist; in fact, was straight-out communism. I looked
down at my covert neighbor and asked, "Do you know what's
happening here...say the NY Times got hold of it?"

He gave me the blankest of dead pan stares..."It
happens all the time," sez he. This was cold war Hollywood
humor, Dr. Strangelove, and I was living it.

To top it off, you've never seen skinnier adults than
these NY suffering socialists. They looked like they hadn't
eaten in weeks, depriving themselves by design of food here
in bountiful America. Well, I'll tell you...the platters they
each carried from the buffet table were stacked about a foot
high. These skinny folks staggered under the weight of a
good capitalist meal. Can you imagine this properly cast and
scripted? Dr. Strangelove for sure.

CRASHING THE CIA MAIN GATE
THE EARLY 1990S

Well, not exactly crashing. Just
knowing which buttons to push.

Coming from Washington's airport to our house, out
Route 123, the entry to the CIA was just a quick turnoff
before ours. An easy mistake to make, just bear right too

soon. I always wondered what would happen if, unwittingly, someone wandered in. So I decided to try it.

That evening I'd picked up four can you believe Polish guys at the airport, my friend Marek Lach and three colleagues all visiting here on a sort of business trip. None knew the States at all. Back then Poland had known but a few years of freedom from the Soviets, and overseas travel was a very special thing. I thought...hm...how 'bout a treat? No idea what would happen.

From the time of our own revolution up to 1990, Poland had no nation of its own except for the 18 years between the two World Wars. It had been divided, repeatedly, between Germany, Austria-Hungary, Russia and lastly the USSR. The world's worst geographic location, Poland.

So without even slowing down I zipped past the guard shack and headed straight for the CIA main parking lot. I knew of course that visitors were supposed to stop and be vetted but I figured what the hell mistakes can be made.

Well. In about 3 seconds we were blocked by 39 huge trucks and surrounded by 412 special police cars, all with bright lights in our faces, a million sirens and drawn weapons. My guests must have thought they'd been trapped...or were somewhere back in not-so-happy Soviet times, about three years past as I remember. It was momentarily exciting.

I was so convincingly innocent and apologetic. We left under escort.

CIA JOB INTERVIEWS

As a young man and young father, in the 1960s, I had good jobs, very good in fact. My first, just out of the army, was with Johns Hopkins, and from there to a succession of federal and private sector jobs... on the US Army general staff as a senior civil servant, at 35, then up to the Office of the Defense Secretary; next a partner in a quite well known consulting firm; and more.

Still I was always looking.

Back in those same 1960s, with my job at Hopkins and in the midst of the most dangerous time of the cold war, everything we did was very highly classified. I had the security clearances. So, I thought, why not try the Agency? I didn't bother to consider that there were few good jobs available; that those were hot Washington jobs...and certainly nothing spy-like for a young family man. Nor did I realize the silly process took many months. I wrote a letter and finally got invited in.

The initial interview took place in an office in a downtown Washington plush neighborhood right opposite the Washington Hilton, on 16th Street. Enter the unmarked door of a townhouse you'd die for, and make your way through one empty office after another and finally meet someone who spoke. I was far too qualified. I got no offer.

There was no doubt that a thousand cameras were trained on that front door from the Soviet embassy, sitting directly across posh 16th street. No doubt. What a joke.

MY NEXT CIA DEAL I REALLY BLEW...NATIONAL INTELLIGENCE OFFICER FOR EUROPE

It was years later and I'd made a kind of name for myself in the Defense Department in European, especially NATO, affairs.

My highly placed neighbor of the wedding was still across the street. He set me up for an interview.

There were at the time eight National Intelligence Officers (NIOs)...just eight. One for each of eight global geographic regions. The job, for each, was to gather, sift and prioritize for the Director and White House all the intelligence for their specific global region. It was a dream opening...the NIO for Europe needed filling. The hottest of regions. And I was a Europe specialist.

I sailed through the first interview. The next was to be with the Agency deputy director, an appointee, a Yale professor, Dr. Robert Bowie. I declined, with the weakest of personal reasons. Back then I still thought folks knew everything of substance they had to know about jobs being interviewed for. This was patently nonsense. Hardly anyone in Washington did!! No bright person ever takes a job for which he or she is really qualified; nothing could be learned from this.

The job had three aspects...one should know the military in all countries...I did. Should know the economics...I most certainly did. And should know the politics, which with 573 Italian political parties, 342 French, and like numbers in other nations...this might take some sorting out. I might have needed a few days. I backed away. Exceedingly foolish of me.

CIA NEIGHBORS

We'd moved from Maryland to be closer to my Pentagon job, bigger home and all that. Had no idea this town, McLean, in northern Virginia, was full of people whom you might never meet...or whose names were whatever the hell they wanted on any given day. We had on our street at least four never meets, coverts who might show up on dark nights in dark cars. A few whose covers were transparent. At least one quite high up and proud of it (you've met him at the wedding above). At least one who'd had the job of handling Soviet defectors...case officers they were called, weren't they? What a happy street.

We also had a safe house and handler for one absolutely top Soviet defector.

And one internal security guy...a truly sad story. Closely watched his own CIA people. That was his job. We'd heard mention of him but had never seen him. His wife, yes, not him. They lived behind us, a high fence. Valerina and William Taut.

One Christmastime evening, cold as can be, a sharp knock on our front door. I open it; a stranger says..."I'm Will Taut. I'd like a double scotch." That's all he said. I said c'mon in, sure. Three double scotches later he left. Three weeks later he died...of cirrhosis of the liver.

Those were days of hard drinking in the sneak business.

THE CLOAK AND DAGGER MAN

This is just a quickee. It was about 1963, my very early days in Washington. We were walking through Georgetown, on lunch break, on a 95 degree Washington July day. Real hot and sweaty.

A tiny sports car pulls up next to us. The door opens and a man, wearing a 1940s brimmed hat, a long heavy winter type coat, collar up and sun glasses, gets out. He walks away, at a quite normal pace.

No movie cameras, nothing. We all looked. Guy was either quite sick or dry running a CIA interview.

THE WONDERFUL JOHN LE CARRE – A FAR LONGER STORY AND FINE BIOGRAPHY

Hard as it may be to believe, this is also true. John le Carre has averred many, many, many times he did not spy. So tell me...what were MI5 and MI6? He worked for both. Did and supervised drops, ran agents, and more...if his Madsen biography is to be believed. Was this so literate man a clerk? Not a spy? Maybe. An agent...you betcha.

The British secret service, post war, was a porous joke. Hard workers, brilliant people as with le Carre...but a continuing lot of defectors and double agents. Must have been a fun place to work. I really would have enjoyed their clubs. Wait a sec...no women were allowed. No wonder there were defectors.

AN EARLY SECRET MISSION

This was not CIA and I can't say where. But was just totally ridiculous as it played through.

It was about 1977 and US-Soviet relations were as tense as ever. I had one of my NATO related jobs, this time focused on the south of NATO; specifically Greece and Turkey and the roles that each should have in blocking any Soviet move to the south. My task was to do a comprehensive assessment of Turkey's armed forces, strengths and weaknesses.

There was then, and remains to this day, deep animosity between these two NATO partners. Refugees, migrants, Cyprus, many wars over time.

We wise people in Washington wished to strengthen Turkey. But our Greek partners fought tooth and nail; said not on your life.

For anything to happen we needed our Congress to lift a long-standing embargo on shipping US arms to the Turks. Again, the Greek lobby dug in, fought like only lobbyists can fight; with much money.

Well...I completed my job. It was obvious, actually. Turkey was flush with troops and WWI rifles, but barely any modern artillery, tanks or aircraft. The silly report was actually classified top secret, as I recall. At least secret, the next lower category.

We needed to get this report to Congress, to make it clear that the embargo had to be lifted. A vote on the embargo was scheduled.

So my boss said to me...shhh...but how about you carrying a copy over there? I thought sure why the hell not. A good boss in fact.

I did. Took a taxi one evening and met some Senate aide on a dark street corner and slipped him this classified report. No receipts or anything legal.

The Senate vote was taken about a week later and we won by three votes; the embargo was lifted, arms would flow, and Greece would be very angry.

I got a special award for this totally unlawful leak. The irony was that the document could have been sent by the usual courier. But no, author must deliver. Nuts.

THE LATEST SECRET MISSION

Like so many who have served our country I have the deepest respect for the Agency. On request I have deleted my reporting of this series of events. But please take my word for it; it will affect our national security. Stay tuned if you can. Presidential perfidy.

Below is a photo, in Edwynystan, of the author with the newly installed Head of State and Chief of Homeland Security.

Tales of the US Army

1959 - How to get love from a "superior" officer

As a young first lieutenant I, along with another first lieutenant, was given responsibility for "firing range" safety at White Sands Missile Range in New Mexico. We were the training ground for the firing of the Army's latest air defense missiles...back during cold war times. Army units stationed both in the US and Europe, protecting major cities and other installations, came each year to practice and be graded. Without a good grade, the major or lieutenant colonel commanding was guaranteed a quick ticket to civilian life.

Our job was to stop any wayward missile..huge guided missiles...from bending back toward El Paso or Mexico's Ciudad Juarez. But we had a never ending problem. Communication to and at the firing sites, up to ten miles away, was by thin wire stretching over the New Mexico desert. The jackrabbits were always chewing it up. Yum, yum. Leaving us no way of ordering a stop!!!

One lieutenant colonel, stationed near an important German city, was always on our case, blaming us lieutenants for the damn desert rabbits. His career hung in the balance, who could blame him? One time after he chewed us out big time, I turned to my buddy Leo, the other lieutenant, and said...enough!

All wires connected, by site number, to a terminal beneath my desk. Remember, this was years ago.

I reached down and disconnected him. A court martial offense, actually. Within minutes the commercial phone outside rang. It was the colonel...steaming. I mean...pissed.

I got to the phone, assured him we had our best people working on it. I signaled up to Leo who then connected up his wires...and told him I thought we had it fixed already. We did.

The colonel officially commended us lieutenants.

I should have turned this over to the MASH writers. Me Hawkeye. Leo Trapper, the colonel Major Frank Burns.

SNAKES R US

The countryside, west Texas and New Mexico, looked bleak to us easterners but was of course very much alive. Coyotes, jackrabbits were everywhere...along with all manner of small creatures and birds. We saw no cougar or jaguar...apparently they stayed up in mountains to the north, or south toward Mexico. But it was snake heaven.

I recall climbing a rock strewn and very steep and extensive hillside one time. This was actually in Oklahoma a few years earlier, in ROTC summer training, but fits the story line.

We mindless officer candidates were being "taught" to read topographical maps; you know...close together lines means steep, far apart lines means flat terrain. We were told to go from here to there and return to our starting point. Anyone who cared and could read could just walk a far apart line all the way and back...no hills at all!

Well...need I tell you? I figured, egotist that I was, that I could go over top and still beat everyone back. There were some really sad characters in my group and I was in super college shape. Two hours later I was still climbing, hand over hand, looking for grab holds. Very steep, just me alone and whatever might lie on the rock above that I grabbed. Three hours later same.

Four hours later I made it back. All but one other fool had beaten me by hours, and no one knew where I was. Yes...I was hit by a rattler and....

Just kidding, but I might have been.

In Texas, where I was later stationed...the colonel story above...I had the duty one night. Had to guard the missile sites from ETs or Soviet drop-ins. Were we paranoid?

Driving about in a jeep that night we killed a rattler. Really upsets me now. I brought it home and draped it on our fence. Called Charley, our young Doberman, over and showed it to him. He looked at me in the way Dobies do and ignored it. What do you think I am he said...stupid?

Well, not to be put off or beaten...I thought of the young officer in our headquarters back at White Sands. His name, truly, was Jimmy Carter and in fact he was from

Georgia...just a coincidence. He feared snakes, we all knew. I just didn't know how much.

I brought the dead snake in next morning early, and slipped it into his desk drawer. Like it was scripted, he arrived, sat down...and opened that drawer. He jumped up screaming and ran out of the building. Another court martial offense. But somehow nothing bad was done to me. Don't know why.

I also just had to make off with the headquarters coffee pot. If you've not been in military service you can't possibly appreciate how important coffee is. It takes the place of having any work...you just fill your cup for the 50th time and look wise or busy.

This was a huge mess hall coffee maker, maybe a yard tall. One of my guys grabbed it and walked out to our Jeep... like he was going to have it repaired. Off we went. About 15 minutes later my phone rang and the major said...Lieutenant Wittner, do you have our coffee pot in your office? I said no.

It was outside. Somehow I got away with this also.

One more army snake story. I had a Philippino master sergeant working for me, a veteran of over 30 years' service including WWII. The Philippines. A few snakes you think? Cobras plus many more, actually.

I'd had my guys steal some contractor equipment one dark night...third court martial offense...and build us a communications shack down the hill from Range Control, from my own office. This combat veteran, from a snake-infested island nation, came screaming up the hill next morning. He'd seen a rattler.

A Virginia snake story...not Army but also fits here -

McLean, Virginia. Suburbia to the hilt. I was walking Bonnie and Petey, our Lab-Hound twins, in the Burling county park...big woods for a suburb. I looked ahead a bit and they, together, had stopped and were circling in a tight bounce. I warned them to back off and hustled up to see what they were up to.

They had spied a snake, ensnared in that Godawful landscaping mesh designed to keep down erosion or keep mulch in place. Or something. It's no more than a permanent blight when placed in the woods. It's made of some "forever" synthetic fabric...what else? It has a grid size of about an inch or so, perfect for catching a fox or coon foot.

Here the snake had tried to crawl through but having no reverse gear it got stuck maybe halfway down its some four feet length. It was quite obviously at first glance a copperhead, not at all uncommon in Virginia. (Later we found one right outside our house on a warm pavement.)

Well, what to do? Bonnie and Pete were standing safely clear and watching. I sure was not about to leave it to die.

I had with me a long-bladed knife. With a stick I held the snake in place and went about cutting the mesh right at the point where it grabbed. I then picked up the snake and walked it on the trail back to my car. People scattered, actually ran off the trail.

There I pointed it toward the park ranger station. I carefully instructed it to bite anyone in uniform. It wagged its tail and took off.

STORIES OF
RED CANYON RANGE CAMP

At the very north end of White Sands Missile Range, the nation's largest landlocked missile test range, lay the Red Canyon Range Camp. All of this was in New Mexico. This was, not incidentally, where the first atomic devices were tested...that was more toward the southern end.

My job, in addition to being Range Safety Officer as described above in the Colonel story, was to brief distinguished visitors on the incredible protection provided to cities and other sites by these very early...and not too reliable...anti-aircraft guided missiles.

We had many mayors and other officials, and senior generals from all our allies back then...German, British, South Korean and more. All coming to see an impressive firing and be briefed. PR stuff of course.

One particular time...our government was pitching an important ally on the value of the missiles sites (meaning please buy some of our equipment…"tied aid"...we give you military aid, taxpayer money, and you then buy our stuff).

So I'm standing there, in front of this august group, headphones on...listening to the launch crew describing

lift off, reaching altitude...and then I waited...and waited...
and waited. All communications had gone dead. High tech
we were not, ordinary 1950s cheap desert wires running to
where I stood. My usual gig was to simply repeat all that was
told to me describing the flight.

But this time nothing but silence and with so many
distinguished eyes all on me...supposedly describing the flight
of this killer bee...at some 30,000 feet.

I had two choices...I could own up to abject technical
failure and face the demise of US foreign policy. Or...I could
fake it.

So...I faked it. As if I was actually hearing. I had it all
memorized line for line by this time, all of some 4 minutes...
right down to hitting the drone target at 30,000 feet some 50
miles away. I knew these words well, what to say after dozens
of these briefings. "We have impact," I said. Flash...you could
see the explosion.

Can you imagine? Suppose the damn thing had
failed...and I had lied? I wonder...would I have been knighted
for creative effort or jailed for deceiving a Korean general?

When I first reported to Red Canyon, as a brand new
first lieutenant right from army rocketry and guided missile
school, I wondered as do most fresh-faced lieutenants. These
army guys, officer and enlisted, had, back then, mostly seen
WWII combat service. Combat veterans in all probability...
real honest-to-God combat. How would they greet, much less
accept, a new guy with two Ivy league degrees?

I found out like fast.

My new boss was Lt. Colonel John J. McCarthy, as Irish as could be and from Brooklyn. I'd barely said hello and saluted. He said, "Lieutenant, we've a real problem here; we fire tomorrow and we've got cattle all over the range." Can you imagine, he said, what it would do to our neighbors up here...and our good friendly relations...if we killed a couple dozen of their cows by accident?

"I want you to get out there," he said, "round them up, and get them off the range." A few dozen he thought. He downed a shot of something...actually a second shot in those maybe total of 15 minutes.

Well. Have you been to northern New Mexico in December? Thirty degrees or below? Wind. Snow. A bit cool.

He assigned some poor sergeant who must've been in the dog house for something to be my driver. We got a jeep, and drove off into the high desert. Pitch black. Gloves, heavy coats, facial cover...whatever I could pile on. It was all I could do to not fall out; bump after bump after ditch.

We found cows everywhere. We'd get behind 3 or 4 and run them. They'd split and we'd end up behind none. They had played this game before. They kept this up for a couple of hours. Me...I was just a new fuzz face. But that poor sergeant driver.

It finally dawned on me that I was being had. I told my driver to go back in before we died...he'd borne this like a real trooper...whatever the hell he did to merit this torture.

It wasn't that much warmer back in the camp headquarters shed. My good colonel was hunkered down by a fire...he and one or two other officers. I don't recall how

much booze was on display...but a lot. He was bombed; this
a really bottom type assignment for any officer...and he had
drawn the short straw.

He said, "Welcome Lieutenant, have a drink." He
admitted this was a fraternal ritual, and broke up laughing. I
was now in the fraternity he said. The sergeant...he just left
us. Nice.

Try driving in an open jeep in high desert in
midwinter.

We had other creatures at this camp. Thousands of
tarantulas in season, scorpions, snakes of course when warm,
deer and bear. But so what? I'd love to have a second home
there now.

One time the road outside camp and for what seemed
acres around was just covered in tarantulas. Crunchy. Pretty
disgusting. Must have been one great party.

In camp we had a mascot. A mule named Nike. Dad
was a well known bon vivant donkey. Mom was a small
but not very nice lady horse. This pet mule just hung out,
wandering around. Usually heading toward people...us or
visitors...anyone who might have a handout.

One time he showed up just behind me as I was
briefing another missile firing. We had a mixed group...men
and women from outside a big eastern city being protected by
our Nike missiles. I think it was Washington actually.

He was just a few yards behind as I spoke to our
visitors...telling them they were so safe and just watch! I lost

their attention. We knew he was oversexed but what he did I cannot tell you.

AIR FORCE AIRCRAFT AND JEWISH WEDDINGS

Early in this army hitch I had occasion to get back East. Big occasion actually. I'd about decided to ask my later wife to marry me. She was as nice and pretty as could be, sharp, and from a good local family. Being military I could fly any Air Force plane that had space.

From Biggs Air Force Base, right in El Paso, I grabbed a flight to San Antonio. A general's airplane, a Lockheed Lodestar...small two-engined runabout for any Air Force senior official. My travelling companions? Two pilots and an incredibly full load of tropical fish in huge tanks. I figured these were good pilots, soft landing guaranteed.

But I still had to get to New York. It was mid-winter. Whatever would be would.

I found a flight heading toward Massachusetts. Air Force converted B26 bomber. Old and slow by today's measure anyway. But the Air Force, then as now, flew. Pretty great guys.

Yep, they flew.

No airplane had landed on the east coast, they told me, in two days...snow and ice. But, they said, they had a party to get to. We landed at Hanscom Field in Massachusetts in a foot of snow. Just another day at work.

THE WEDDING...

For the service we booked my in-laws' favorite local rabbi. I had little interest then, nor did my parents. Even though first generation Americans and children of religious immigrants, they passed on to me a healthy respect for religions in general but not much interest in things done for the sake of tradition.

My European roots were, and remain, extremely important to me, as discussed in Part II of this book, but no interest at all in rote obedience. If anything, now, in my old age, I'm a deist. I have good company...both Voltaire and Einstein, from my readings, tended this way.

This rabbi was a local New York deity himself. Impossible, now, to even understand why so many looked up to him. But people did, as many now do to others. He was a big man with heavy features and he made absolutely certain to stand up very close to us. In our faces actually. I guessed so he might pass on special advice.

He spat, corrected himself many times.... It was just awful.

Maybe ten years later it came out that he had been having a long-term affair with his secretary. Horror of horrors in the community. Kinda nice to know rabbis can be human, but what an incredible phony. He disappeared to somewhere.

SPORTS AND OTHER ASSORTED STORIES

FISHING STORIES

A few fish tales.

I loved fishing from about age 8; Rockaway Beach lies between the ocean and Jamaica Bay at the southwestern tip of Long Island. I recall vividly my father taking me for my first very own fishing rod and reel. The cost was $8.00. I told him it was the luckiest day of my whole life. Wonder how he felt?

I pretty quickly began to bring home the large summer flounder locally known as fluke, porgies and other great eating fish. They were appreciated, we weren't flush with money. In my early teens I graduated to surf casting. I went some time learning to enjoy solitude and no fish, which is the way of surf casting. But then the striped bass and big bluefish found me and the walk home became a good thing for a proud kid.

But let's move on. I was crazy about the open ocean water even back then. I read and re-read, every author... Joe Brooks, George Reiger, a guy named Hemingway, Lefty Kreh...many more. Florida, the Bahamas, Hawaii were my dreams. I wondered...is it really possible to catch fish of God knows...1000 pounds?

I have not. About 200 pounds is still my tops, a bull shark we released.

Ocean City, Maryland and Cape Hatteras

For about three years I actually did my time, in season, as a kind of first mate. An Army friend, Colonel Bill Laurence, had a 25 foot diesel, much overpowered. A great guy, Vietnam vet, a pilot, drank a ton and smoked cigars while inhaling diesel fumes blow back. Service fliers, all services, can be a pain, do pretty much what they wish. Maybe not Navy, the guys I knew were sane. Had to be sane to land on a carrier. Air Force and Army fliers...watch out.

But I learned baits and rigging and small boat handling. We went 50 miles offshore almost every time, to the canyons...the deep underwater drop-offs. Three hour run each way for maybe 4 hours fishing, in good weather. Amazingly, our first season, we took third in the first ever Ocean City White Marlin tournament, a contest now offering millions of dollars in prize money. Sixty-one pound white marlin we took. Whites are not really big.

The only blue I ever heard about while fishing was a captain's rumor. Off Hatteras, our captain screamed, "It's a blue one, a blue one!!" Never saw it. Possibly only a shark. The captain's name I remember...Buddy Canady or something like that. Long-time Carolina fishing family. I did get to see, but only in an ice house, the then world record 1200 pound blue marlin. That was a large fish.

On the island of Hawaii, one time, I did see a pickup truck absolutely loaded with blue marlin. It was a shocker... they ate those? I guess so.

I went out one time with a couple of commercial guys, also from the Kona coast. They had a small boat and did much handlining...heavy handlining. I'd hoped for tuna...or anything... just to see it happen as locals did. No action at all that day.

THE EARL OF HATTERAS

We were headed out, 6 am one day, from Oregon Inlet, just north of Hatteras. This made for a shorter run, some 20 to 30 miles and we'd be fishing. The boats leaving the inlet were lined up that morning, in file. Looking aft it looked like the Japanese navy for maybe a half mile, heading out to battle.

I was in the first mate role as usual, while Bill drove the boat and smoked cigars. We had two guys from the Jersey shore as guests, experienced fisherman they said.

We'd all had the standard early morning macho breakfast..me six cups of coffee, three orders of bacon, and a double order of 6 pancakes syrup smothered. A nice light breakfast, good for offshore.

We were actually targeting blue marlin or big sharks, such that I had to rig big baits. Whole squid, slimy as might be, maybe 20 inches tip to tip. Pretty nasty. So there I was, bent over the rigging table, just aft of the steering console. Diesel fumes, Bill's cigar smoke...and me having had a totally crazy breakfast.

About a half hour out it hit me. All was about to come up. The noise I made as I rushed to the transom to upchuck was something like... "errrrrrrrrllll."

So I became the Earl of Hatteras. We caught one wahoo that day, that was it. But the Jersey boys had fished with the Earl of Hatteras.

WHITE MARLIN ONE, US NOTHING

This was off Ocean City, Maryland, that much longer run to the fishing grounds.

We'd trolled and searched all day without so much as seeing any fish at all, and started to head home. Gorgeous clear late afternoon.

These offshore boats have what are called outriggers, tall aluminum or alloy poles designed to lie out to the port and starboard sides and keep the lines from getting entangled. They can be maybe 30 feet long on the bigger boats...for some reason our 25 footer had these over-long riggers. Each rigger has support wire bracing to minimize whipping around, to prevent a possible snapping.

Well...we're heading in at speed and the support wiring on the starboard rigger pops. Bill throttles back fast, I get up on the side and wrestle the rigger out...it was heavy... and dump it in the boat for repair. We sit, just rolling gently. We've seen not one fish all day.

You guessed it...a white marlin, easily identified by the round dorsal, comes up alongside, stares sideways at us, and circles round the boat 2 or 3 times...very slowly. We could see what he was saying...you guys are idiots, can't catch a fish and bust up your boat. Get outta here while you can. We did.

FLORIDA

In my job, earlier, I'd met a guy whom others described as the fisherman of all Florida fisherman. He was an engineer, but had grown up on the Florida east coast fishing...starting at age five he later told me. From the lower Keys north to Jupiter, from what I learned.

His name I will keep a secret...but I'll tell you that he, in my later years, made all my fishing dreams come almost true... almost because I've never really sought out striped, blue or black marlin and don't really care anymore. I now wish they'd all be left in their ocean, unbothered by man...a forlorn hope of course.

He took me and my grandsons out several times, charging me very little even though he was commercially

Sarasota, Florida

licensed. We caught our own bait and hardly be out of the
inlet...and the fish were on us. Name the species, he knew
where they all lived...from very shallow to very deep water.

One day I asked for a sailfish, for my grandsons, and
we had one by 8:45 am. Another day he and I sought smaller
eating fish, which he could sell. For hours we wrestled up
all manner of snapper and whatever. Over 200. He sold
them; I went back to the motel my head and the motel badly
spinning.

Only once did he break off a fish. We were fishing
deep and a grouper, albacore...something...grabbed hold and
he knew on ten pound test no way...why waste time.

It was on this boat that we brought boatside that 200
pound bull shark, immediately released.

He also has the most wonderful collection of shell and fin fish, mounted by himself, imaginable. At least two full room walls. I hope to see this again. And maybe fish.

Thank you...Dave K.

BASEBALL

These must start with my college experience, because I never knew what I could do. No baseball in high school for me; all high school sports were cancelled my last two years due to teacher labor issues...all extracurricular activities in fact were dropped.

I had tried to make the Cornell basketball team, but was the last guy cut. Actually after the season started. It was a good cut, I never would have played. But I came to know the coaches, one of whom was also the baseball coach. I already loved the sport; loved all New York teams...the Dodgers, Yankees and especially the Giants.

So come spring, with temperatures way up to about 35 degrees in central New York, I went for baseball. Unbelievably, in a couple weeks, that same coach told me I had a future in professional baseball if I cared enough.

I did shortstop, the only position that interested me, but with a special skill at anticipating where the batted ball would be hit I covered lots of ground. I myself could hit as well.

Looking back now, my parents gave me great eyes and more, including this ability to see ahead. One time I got directly behind the second baseman and turned his error into an out at first.

Ah...memories.

But this was an Ivy league school. I was there for an education. And it was an Ivy league coach who said what he said, not a New York Yankee coach.

I hurt myself a little later anyhow, separating a shoulder, the kind of injury that lingered, making it impossible to bat as I did. Still I stayed with the team for three years, having fun.

That injury, by the way, got me tossed out of Navy ROTC, silly Navy rules. I found out much later I might have appealed. I very much wanted the Navy. The Army said we don't care at all, took me in, I got my commission and we got the stories I tell in this book.

As an aside, I very nearly got a full Navy scholarship to Cornell. I heard later I should have worn a tie to the interview. My parents must have loved me for this early show of independence. Cost them a fortune, the way I managed all this.

Cornell was for education, not baseball. Good grades were tough enough to get. I did not, until my last two years.

......Big gap now in baseball tales.

SENIOR SOFTBALL

How's this for a time warp? A jump from 1955 to 1990?

I went back to baseball, only it was softball, in 1990. Played on a Virginia team, kinda worked my way back in. This senior softball was nonsense compared to baseball..slow pitch, extra outfielder...huge scores.

I did get invited, in Maryland later on, to play in a senior hardball...that is, baseball...so-called all-star game. I had a base hit in my only at bat before the rains, which wasn't too bad after not seeing a baseball pitch for some 45 years. I was the oldest guy by far and I'm thinking if these guys are all-stars then indeed I did miss my career.

One particular softball at bat comes to mind...I hit the longest home run in league history...it took about 20 minutes. I got into a pitch and drove it to the centerfield fence.

All four outfielders started limping after it. I began my limp toward first base. By the time they reached it and threw it in, 20 feet at a time, and I made my way around the bases... twenty minutes had passed.

Another time I did something similar. We were losing 15-0 and I hit another home run. That made it 15-1. The entire dugout came out and hugged me. Unbelievable.

These were my only two homeruns in some 15 years of senior softball. We did win any number of league championships though.

This game got ridiculous. Infielders wore catchers' masks. Soon five infielders as well as the four outfielders and the pitcher soon was protected by a batting practice screen. I was happy to give it up.

SKIING

As my family well knows, I dropped out of a good Washington job and bought a ski lodge and restaurant in New Hampshire. Quite foolish. But my brother had just died, of an ugly cancer, under my care, and I was tired. My mind unnecessarily clouded. I lost a bundle of money on that one but did get in some nice skiing.

Back in Virginia we did have some local skiing...if you liked ice. One time I was in training for the local ski patrol... Massanutten it was.

I was first to come upon a real injury one Saturday, a woman had hurt her leg, clearly needed help. I stopped, crossed my skis upright to summon help and the toboggan.

My compatriot, another trainee, and a physician, came barreling down and skied into her. I then twisted her bad knee lifting her. I bet she needed psychiatric help more than orthopedic.

Another time they placed a "victim", a pretty girl of about 20, off to the side. I was to be graded, this was final exam time. She told me she had bad problems in her legs; I was to determine where and how bad. No thanks. The patrol guy with the watch, timing me, about died laughing; no way I would touch her.

I failed. But catch this aftermath.

Exactly ten days later, on my way to work, the car ahead of me drove off the road smack into the end of a stone retaining wall. Dead stop, no slowing down. I was first to get back to him.

I recognized the driver immediately, an army major I worked with. Hunched over the wheel, semi conscious, right foot all but torn off. I dragged him out and away, fearing explosion.

Soon others came along to help, including a doctor, and I, a bit shaken, continued to work. I called in the accident to his office.

Interesting? I fail a ski patrol exam and get the real thing within days?

Was someone upstairs watching?

More stories? Part II next after Lord Rockaway.

LORD ROCKAWAY
OF DOWNTON ABBEY

This is he. A perfect specimen of an Appenzell-Eltebuch Swiss mountain dog. More Eltebuch actually. Not kidding, check it out.

By way of lead in to Part II of this book, which was keynoted by dogs, let me tell you of Rocky. (The first two Part II stories are of Dipper the Foxhound, and Petey and Bonnie.)

He came to us at age 7, two years after Dipper died. We waited, not sure...did we or not? I mean...16 years of foxhound singing and who cares attitude. She was a pleasure but only by her rules.

And we waited too long to "put her down"...that awful expression...by at least six months. But we all do that, don't we? Keep a beloved animal alive for us...not him or her??

I searched six local shelters looking for another foxhound. Over my wife's objections. She felt they smelled, which they do, and of course they sing at all hours. Sing is better than bay. I found only one at that time and she was young and crazy. Gorgeous, as foxhounds can be, but just no discipline...bananas.

Finally one shelter called us. They had two dogs they wanted us to see. A young "labradoodle" and an older whatever...you see him above. A mix they said. Mary wanted the doodle of course, but the shelter looked at us and said uh uh...she's too young for you guys.

What they meant was we were too old...it was pretty clear. She a bouncing 10 month old and we an average of 78 – not bouncing, hardly moving. (Slight exaggeration.)

Rocky came zooming in to us from an adjoining room. Tennis ball in mouth, stubby tail going like mad. We'd been told he was affectionate. I got down to the floor to meet him. He dropped the tennis ball and proceeded to wash my face. He was then 77 pounds and much overweight. No foxhound this dog. So incredibly loving.

He had a gloriously thick tan, black and some white coat. He resembled a kind of friendly Javelina, were there such a thing. Good age for us, this loving creature.

We were dead meat. Two weeks later he came home.

I changed his official name to Lord Rockaway to commemorate Rockaway Beach where Mary and I grew up and added Downton Abbey because it was then so current and sounded neat.

As I write, he's nine. Down 20 pounds by way of smart feeding. Still a tennis freak. Has about five tennis balls spread around the house. But may I tell you of his character, this whatever maybe Swiss herding dog mix?

Loving all people to a fault. Still checks all new dogs carefully, very much assured and dominant if need be. A little dog talk and he's in charge. Raises a fuss at night if there's any noise outside. Responds to hand signals and whispered requests...like please leave the kitchen...ok? There's got to be herding "to please" in there somewhere.

Rarely needs a leash. Goes to barber shop, greets barber with licks and then lies on floor waiting for me, as in an old movie. Greets Mary and me each day with a million licks. Simply asks to be with us. No more than that.

We did look him up in a huge and very detailed dog book, at the suggestion of a young woman, a neighbor, from Switzerland. His looks and character are of the smallest of the four Swiss Mountain Dogs. The Eltebuch. Really. You can check it.

As my daughter, herself a dog lover, says so often...the perfect dog.

He is that.

M.A.C., Annapolis

PART II

THREE DOGS,
SOME SATIRE,
A GIRL
AND EUROPE

Three Dogs, Some Satire, A Girl and Europe

A.V. Wittner

Stories

Brussels, Bruges and London - 1977;
Food Prepared Finnishly

France and Iceland - 1982; MAD, U.S. Military
Planning and a Wood Carving that Made Up for
Everything

Israel, Paris, Frankfurt and London -1988;
Always Bring Chinese Spare Ribs

1991 - How it Happened - My First Visit to Poland
and Learning Smuggling

Poznan, Poland - June 1991 and *Free*
After Almost 200 Years of Occupation

Italy 1992 - a Girl or a Dog?

Poznan to Warsaw 1992 -
The Importance of a Smooth Bottom

The South of Poland - 1993;
Targeted by a So Tragic Drunk

Warsaw 1996 - Monuments to Heroism

Berlin and Poznan - 1998 and
the Thrill of No Lanes for You

Poznan to Bonn to Paris - 1998;
Driving With Me Not Miss Daisy

Prague 1998 - Number One for Good Reason

Cologne, Bonn and Fulda - 2000;
Deep Underground Travels

Prague 2000 - Once More is Just Fine
and the Marsupial Tea Cup

The Baltic Coast of Germany - 2001;
Simply Personal Not Special

Poznan 2002 - The So Emotional Visit -
Welcome Home from the Polish Colonel

Krakow 2003 - A Special City and
Maybe the Best Most Special City of All

Warsaw to Poznan - 2004;
A Very Bittersweet Taste of Life Past and Present

Munich - 2004: Mad Ludwig You did Good

Frankfurt, Beautiful Heidelberg, First Touch of the
Black Forest, and Pickpocketing Paris Style - 2004

Moscow 2005 - The Air Show, the Metro, No
Evidence of Anything Done Right, Two Incredible
Feasts

2006 - In the Storybook Pretty Black Forest
and on to Strasbourg

2006 - Geneva and Chamonix; The Red Light Hotel,
the Strangest Train Station and a Ski Town of Ski
Towns

May 2007 - The Polish Seacoast,
Beautiful Towns and Seals

THREE DOGS

FOREWORD

We can all write dog stories. So many have in fact. In our family we've had Irish setters, Dobermans, Basset hounds for comic relief, one smallish athletic mixed breed who died, I think now, of undiagnosed Lyme disease, an incredible brother and sister pair, and a sweet very opinionated adopted foxhound. A pretty nice mix.

I write, first, of the last named - she is still with us, now, at eleven and a half (and I'm so terrified of that day that always comes), and then of the brother/sister pair... Petey and Bonnie.

DIPPER THE FOXHOUND

We had just moved into our home in Annapolis, after a transition year in an apartment making up our minds where we wanted to be for this next phase of our lives. This was all a pain, this past sixty moving. We had raised our kids in McLean, Virginia, just outside Washington, but wanted to get away from expense, zillions of cars, and, in my own case, what I felt was the shallowness of our capital city. I guess it was part burnout, after my years of trying to shape government a bit, and of course failing.

From as far back as I can remember I've loved dogs. Especially big dogs. I recall bringing a German shepherd home one day; I was nine or ten I think, and my parents of course launched a search for his home…and found it. Sad me. Why is this, you think? Why do young kids, some anyway, just plug in to dogs? My guess is it's an innate feel for the truest of trusting love, a love between different creatures.

Petey and Bonnie, of whom you will read next, had just passed on, about a year apart. I, of course, nuts about dogs still at age 64 wondered. What to do? I was work commuting back to Washington, an hour plus away, and Mary was working. To get a dog made little sense.

So I went and did it. The local SPCA. No big bucks overbred papered dog for us.

But a foxhound? Of all dogs, a true hunting dog? Well…let me tell you. You try resisting a tricolored… gorgeous brown, white and black…sad brown-eyed, long-eared and smallish female who just sat and watched you, quietly and sweetly, while you decided her fate. Maybe her life or death fate. She wasn't just pretty - she also had a perfect designer spreading cow lick on the back of her neck.

And most deceivingly she uttered not a sound. This was the biggest con job imaginable. She has not shut up since. MacKinley Kantor some years back wrote of Bugle Ann, a foxhound of the hill country, in a beautiful short book called "The Voice of Bugle Ann". Bugle Ann was often allowed to run much of the night, and her voice was unmistakably different from all other hounds who ran with her.

Well, Dippy's is indeed different…from anything I'd ever known. Especially in the car. I could not shut her up and finally got ear plugs, after over ten years. She of course sang on the streets, on her walks, also. She sang for dogs, cats, friends human or not, and the occasional deer or fox. She sang for pure joy. One Sunday, walking in town, some guy sleeping Saturday off at about 11 am, shouted down from a third floor to shut my dog up. I suggested he get up. No way I could, or would, change her.

How did she get her name? Well, we had a neighborhood kid dog-naming contest when she first showed up. Dipstick was the choice. Yep, Dipstick. It might have been her tail, which showed white at the tip but black further down, from checking your oil, or from 101 Dalmations number two. We never knew. But Mary quickly opted for Dipper…and Dippy and Dips…which stuck and fitted her fine.

She had one habit as a young dog we never figured out. She would grab one toy after another and come tumbling

down our basement stairs to where we'd be watching
television; drop the toy and go for another. She just left them
with us. This lady dog, but for the interminable singing,
had no bad habits. She was totally clean and housebroken
from day one with us, at six months, never chewed anything
or stole food, and with gently wagging tail smiled her way
through life.

But here I was, in a water town, with the one dog who
did not swim. My so intrepid outdoor dog would not get her feet
wet!

As the years passed, with many walks in town, in so
pretty Annapolis, Dippy made friends. A million questions…is
that really a foxhound; I've never seen one…was quite common.
Kid after kid wanted to pet this most gentle and sweet, and
singing, lady dog. But her best friends were the Annapolis
shopkeepers. As I write, she has five stores, and storekeeper
managers, who invite her in for a treat. Two actually unlock
their doors, if closed, if Dip stands outside and calls. What a
great and fun thing.

At age eleven and a half she has us totally trained.
Maybe I made a mistake; I gave up on her quite early. She
was but six months when she came to us and I think now
I might have taught her a little something in the way of
manners. Or even some obedience - she's the only dog I've
had whom I've never let run even near the house. I was so
fearful she'd take off and go to foxhound heaven under some
car. As I write, at this moment this elegant and unique lady
dog dozes just behind me in my office. We've just returned
from a walk.

Dip has also been the dog of two of my grandsons, who could not fit their own into their crowded and busy lives. In fact, I chose her partly for that reason - medium sized, pretty and I hoped as I watched her at the shelter...gentle. The boys love her, walk her and fuss over her as I might wish they would. A great thing for all four of us.

Let's just let her doze. I'm so happy I've made her a life with us.

PETE AND BONNIE - A FINAL LESSON

(The original title of this piece was "Pete - My Most Beloved Teacher". It was submitted to my local newspaper which wanted to publish but asked me to cut 300 words from this so terribly drawn out 1100 words. I said, politely of course, forget it. Hope you can wade through it...its soooooo long!)

Dog stories are old hat. You've read one, you've read them all. Maybe.

Pete is over ten now. His sire was a big foxhound, his mom a lab/shepherd cross. He is a tall, rangy, and rugged 75 pounds or so. He runs forever, still, and he swims and thinks. His parents gave him everything wonderful. His sister Bonnie is with us too. She's a smaller, sweeter version. They've been with us since birth almost.

But this is about Petey.

His appearance is remarkable. He is a dappled brown and white, with a strong setter face, eyes far beyond expressive, long limbed, lab ears and a tail of about six inches, curved like an eagle's beak. The tail is the perfect imperfection. It just sets off everything else. He is a show stopper, literally. We cannot walk him without the

*invariable question… "What breed is he?" We answer something like
Tasmanian Boar Hound and get a knowing, "Yes, I know that breed."
Just two days ago, in downtown Annapolis, a man came over, out of
his way, to put his hand down and say only… "Beautiful, beautiful."*

But looks only make you proud.

Here's what he's been for over ten years:

*- At about nine months. He decided to protect me, my car and
my daughters. This big gentle hound pup became my family guardian.
His decision, very early in his life.*

*- At home he never strays from my side. I can't shake him.
He's never more than two feet away. He often tries to press against
me, to touch me. He takes my hand, as dogs do, and just holds it
while gazing into my eyes. He will lick a scratch or cut, not, I believe,
because of the taste but because he thinks his lick will help heal.*

*- In the field or on the beach, he runs ten miles for every one I
walk. But he checks back with me every ten minutes just to be sure I'm
not lost. He has energy, curiosity and enthusiasm for life beyond belief.
Non-stop but not like so many retrievers…he asks questions and seeks
answers.*

*- Amazingly he never fights another dog. He stands and
growls or just steps aside. He whimpers, though, if I deny him the
right to meet and socialize with a new dog. He simply won't fight his
own kind. More than once his sister bailed him out. I wonder…can we
humans learn something from this?*

*- You can't hug him. I can't hug him. If I put my face close to
his, he sounds a gentle warning, a low but serious growl. I don't know
why. It may be that he must do things his own way, even with me.*

- This so serious and purposeful dog has about ten personal toys, including bones, a slipper and a stuffed bear he carries everywhere. It is the height of counterpoint to see him glaring at you over a teddy bear. It just doesn't fit.

- As a young dog, he swam some 200 yards out into the Bay after two geese. You could see the bubble over the geese's heads... "Hey, we got a dumb one this time. Just a little more and he's done!" I turned him, with frantic yelling.

- He caught a squirrel one morning, and I yelled at him from the window to drop his prize. He did, amazingly, and when I went out he was ashamed of himself. I told him he had done two terrific things and we both felt great.

- As a very young dog he would bounce ten feet or so up a tree trunk chasing squirrels. And always land back on his haunches and go up again. It was a glorious, harmless pastime.

- He retrieves, as any retriever, but he really pushes it. He'll retrieve from the ocean and get rolled in the surf. This I had to watch very carefully. He risks broken shoulders, as well as drowning. But I won't deny him. I can't. Maybe if you've surfed, as I have, you understand.

- At home he and Bonnie have learned to open the refrigerator and whichever kitchen drawers smell the best. Actually, we're not sure who does it. We just bungee everything shut.

So for a man who loves dogs as I do, this is a glorious once-in-a-lifetime animal. I could not know what was to happen.

Pete is dead.

Wendy, the author and Mary with a young Dipper

Same Dipstick

Same

Dipper and three nude boys

Dipper on high hound alert

Dipper does dishes

Baird (the author's grandson) and Dipper

*Petey -
A handsome
dog with a
ridiculous
tail*

Sunday morning at home with Bonnie and Petey

*Petey and
Bonnie -
brother and
sister profiles*

He died, just a month short of eleven, of a seizure or heart attack while running with me and his sister. He died as he should, while doing what he loved so terribly much. And I, who loved him, was with him. But why then? Was this planned? I'm not really a religious man, but here's what happened.

About five years before, my family and I entered a time of real stress. It was mostly of my doing, but whatever the cause it was very real. And it fell unto me to do what I could to make things better for all of us. It was rough and very draining.

But perhaps God, in His wisdom, gave me something that made it possible for me to never flag in my efforts, to not let up for a moment. He gave me a dog who had no speed but all out all day and all night, who would look at me and say "Ok, do it and do it now. Don't quit, do it!"

Pete has been dead since early the morning of April 3rd. Three days later, driving home from work grieving more than any rational person should over a dog, and knowing so many people who had experienced real tragedy to which this did not compare, it dawned on me why I had this terrible hole in my heart and gut.

This dog loved me so much he became the best teacher of my life. He taught me to never let up if indeed the search was for something good and decent. He was taken just one month after our personal crisis ended.

He had done his job.

Some Satire

Non-Universal Suffrage and World Peace

Many of us take great pride in our universal suffrage, even though our founders didn't think much of the idea. It did, after all, take a constitutional amendment to make it happen; it didn't seem so wise when we, upstarts and insurgents that we were, threw the British out. Were the Jeffersons and the like onto something? Is such suffrage likely to increase the chance of unhappy involvement in overseas scrapping? In unwise projection of military force? Actually, it seems so, since in a statistical sense nations that restrict the right to vote pretty much live quietly and in peace. Like the oil nations, as examples.

Let's not debate that. One certainly can't trust statistics.

But let's look at a different system. One that would allow voting as a function of achievement, of religion, of education, of height and weight and of other factors but not of gender.

Let us propose a voting range of from one fifth to ten times the standard "one vote". Outlined below is how it would work. If an individual were to fall in more than one category, which will happen often, he or she will be placed by his or her mother-in-law, with no appeal allowed.

First, those with advanced education, a masters or PhD, will be allowed but .5 of a vote. We all know how they would vote. This telegraphing of vote is simply not allowable. Beyond this it gets perfectly logical and easy:

Elementary education only	- 1 vote
High school	- 2 votes
Religious zealot	- .5 vote (same reason as advanced degree holders)
Owner of pickup	- 2 votes
Owner of Hummer	- disenfranchised
Owner of Volt-to-be	- 3 votes
Successful in business	- 1 vote
Very as above	- 5 votes
Very tall	- 3 votes (sports are our lifeblood)
Very fat	- undecided; too busy anyhow
Agnostic	- must abstain
Musician	- 8 votes
Dog lover	- 2 votes
Cat lover	- .3 vote
Closet Libertarian	- 10 votes

Other categories are being considered. Write in or write your Congressperson.

The basic beauty of this is that it will so confuse the electoral college that results will not be known until time has come for the next election.

THE SECRET TRUTH ABOUT PAMPLONA 1980 BUT NOT IRAQ 2006

There we were, back in 1980, in France again and with time to spare. And it was July, a bit hot. So why not check out Spain, couldn't be much hotter. In fact the Basque country of the north might even be cooler. I might discover a new kind of humongous dog I could surprise my wife and vet with. The Basque country was relatively peaceful right then.

On July the 7th of course the bulls run in Pamplona. Hemingway reported this to the world in *The Sun Also Rises*, and the world hasn't ever forgiven him. Why if you think of it should anyone but a wallet-inflated tourist even begin to care? The locals OK, it was their macho bit, one way maidens ranked their prospective mates - although I wondered when reading *The Sun* if the fastest (most frightened) or slowest (most clumsy and dumbest) was the better choice, carefully selected, for a mate. Kind of like human peacocks inflating, maybe. Totally a chick thing I would never understand.

Imagine you are the bull keeper and trainer. You gotta get these guys in shape.

"Ok, you bulls, listen up! It's only 2 weeks now. We're starting bull bed check. No bulls on the streets after 10 pm. If you need a date with a cow, let the coaching staff know we'll get you one. And remember no late snorting and reading either. You will (!) be up and at training table by 6 from now on. "

"If you're not in top shape by the 7th you won't catch even one of those brain lame superior beings. Worse, your buddies will run right over your big fat butt. So...this is it! No more gorging on ragweed, no more bull shitting til late at night, no nothing but think chasing down one of those little two legged squirts. Got it?"

This is history channel stuff. You know - that over 70 ex-marine who tells us everything no one needed to know about WWI weapon designers and their favorite breakfast foods, while driving all through Texas in his Hummer.

Ok enough on the bulls. Think now of the Pamplona Runner Club, of those fine minds whose passion it is to be chased through narrow streets by prehistoric monsters. Girls must be very hard to come by. Very tough indeed to impress. A bad town.

A quick word on this Pamplona. It is and has been the county seat of the province of Navarre, in English Never. Established by the Moors in a moment of indecision, it is located at the confluence of the north flowing (oddly upgrade) Berber river and the south flowing Morroes. This geologic confusion some say lies at the heart of all this.

Bulls are no longer indigenous, they are imported for this festival from Mexico and even France. Again, this may offer a key insight; local bulls all vamoosed years ago. The town has but one street, thereby keeping the need for navigational Onstar-like skills and thought on both sides to a minimum.

Now back to the local cross country club. Only one street so no turns to challenge your mind, playboy maidens to be had, imported second class bulls. Just run straight and fast, you get your choice of chick. Here they are with their coach.

"It's Bulllllll time again!! And this year we got so many beautiful, new, sexy…uh…chicks in town! From everywhere this year even Brooklyn Tech and a few from you guessed it Lincoln (or Tilden; all high schools in Brooklyn)! Sooo what you gonna do…run slow and hope to end it fast, or zoom on ahead and miss out totally?"

Strategy was not his forte, this coach. He sat down with another glass of local red wine, same color as his toes. A few of the…brighter…guys did line up facing the wrong way and the survivors did get first crack at the women.

No one really knows about Pamplona. I mean lots of places have dumb local traditions, funny Mardi Gras type holiday costumes being the least ludicrous. But being chased by 1500 pounds of bad breath has got to be vacant. I can say this, critically, because we have no odd doings in our country these days of Iraq. None at all. Especially none at the top.

Would Bush strut down Pamplona's only street declaring victory? We can hope so.

Well, we saw it, we watched it and no one got more than a few thru body thrusts or stomped on more than twice above the shoulders. At least not that we know. The head injuries went unreported to the press and were nowhere near serious in net effect. Couldn't be. The runners had begun brain dead.

Women? A myth. The prizes were 68 year old German and American tourists.

Forget the bulls and the other misguided males. Go off season. From my biased viewpoint just another silly way some of mankind demonstrate their incontestable inferiority to animals. I wish the bulls all the best in the future and will certainly give what I can if it may add wins to the bull cause. I think the NFL surely has a place here. Footwork and thought. Big playbook.

The Basque food and countryside...the best! So go.

If only I might write something like this of Iraq. But no parody is possible.

Another Secret Truth - Texas and The Black Forest

In the far southwest of Germany on the Swiss and French borders lies the sub-state of Baden. It isn't exactly a state like the major states such as North Rheine Westphalia or Bavaria. It lies within a real state...Wurttemburg. Sometimes it is called Baden Wurttemburg. Confused?

But in those even more confused times when Germany was but dozens of princely rulings over thousands of hectares, as just after the Congress of Vienna after Napoleon in 1815, it was a state. Or it was called such.

Who cares anyhow.

It lies in for my money the prettiest part of the entire country, the Black Forest or Schwarzwald - a region of gentle mountains up to about 4000 feet and beautiful valleys. It lies also next to Alsace, the part of current day France that had been one most bitterly disputed parts of the German-French borderlands. *It's kind of where the Alps decided to settle down.* I'll point you to this region later when speaking of Heidelberg. Rolling, story book pretty villages.

In that ancient time, the 1800's, no one wanted Baden. Or everyone wanted Baden. It changed hands or more accurately princes whenever force of arms made it so. Treaties were sometimes written, more often not. Baden just was in or out of something else, didn't seem to matter much.

Not many realize this but Texas has a similar history. No one wanted Texas either.

In a little known footnote to the ending of our war with Mexico, in the late 1840s, Mexico, having fought hard but deciding to capitulate, managed to ring in a treaty provision that has been largely overlooked by historians. The U.S. was told look we can continue fighting or you can agree to take Texas off our hands.

Who wanted it? Who needed the aggravation of 40 million square miles of sidewinders and mesquite? No oil hunger then, nothing at all. It was expensive in every way; people even fought over this nothingness. It took on a mystique…gee we gotta have it…but in fact this is a historical falsehood.

Mexico coerced us into taking it by threatening to continue the fight.

Therein lies a lesson. Had we even known Baden existed, with no one fighting hard enough to get rid of it, we might have resisted and not gotten stuck with Texas. The oil? No big deal, we get so much from Mexico anyway.

So that's how we really got Texas.

CNN AND
FOREIGN CORRESPONDENTS

It was, one time in the distant past, that a student might attend college and major in journalism. Back then print journalism exclusively. Occasionally newspaper work was even found for English majors and history majors, who usually could think and write. In the beginning for some lucky few came the highly sought after job title of foreign correspondent. These people were select and so literate.

Very early on it was just print but then came radio and now satellite in your face television journalism.

We all know the progression. In the last century from Hemingway to Ed Murrow and Bill Shirer, to Dan Rather in his not too recent days. Now to the dozens parading around the world and beaming back the most troubling news imaginable to the so hungry viewers desperate to know of things that really ought not to be of too much concern. Things that would not be of concern if unreported and almost always blown up far out of consequence...thereby making news. Wars included, which if under-reported might perhaps have a chance of simmering down.

Please don't misunderstand. I very much admire the people on the ground doing this work.

Alan Furst's most recent book as I write, his jewel in my opinion because it is so clean and quick moving, is called *The Foreign Correspondent.* Those who report in it do so with restraint. They had to do it that way. They used cables and an occasional phone call. No information overload. Can you imagine...just a few facts? No house dressing? The stuff of a sane foreign policy just maybe? No, not naivete on my part. Just wistfulness.

While I don't watch Al Jazeera and can't say for sure, I just know that 99% of what is reported one way or another in the Arab world is no better than what we see and hear here. Total I got it first news, slanted as today's government might wish, or in the West, as today's big bucks sponsor might wish.

I'm trying to make another point, and Marya Mannes, as quoted in a weekly news magazine, made it better than I can. She said, "The more people are reached by mass communication the less they communicate with each other."

So take CNN (please). Or even MSN or Fox depending on your stomach. Wolf Blitzer? Can you imagine…a guy named Wolf yelling at you with the always "just breaking" story? It has to be breaking. Otherwise it would be 38 seconds old.

This guy was born one of identical twins…Alka and Broma. The hospital, probably in Lower Kanjanistan, got it wrong. Or on its own made a correction. But in truth no news broadcaster even with the latest and greatest most agitating news might be called Alka Blitzer. This would be upsetting, not calming, to the stomach Wolf is an improvement for sure. His dad was Whyne, a fixture at all those Long Island summer beach parties.

Ok. Sorry Wolf. Your secret is out.

But I have another problem. I worked for some years in the Pentagon, where one of my bosses was a deputy assistant secretary of defense. Later there came to be associate deputy assistant secretaries and associate deputy assistant under secretaries and now I hear deputy assistants to the associate deputy assistant under deputies. This after President Junior Bush cleaned up the Pentagon personnel system as part of his surgical approach to engaging in combat with the world.

So how come every single correspondent called to the microphone by Wolf and his dear and close colleagues at Fox, MSNBC and even the networks, is...invariably "Our Veteran Senior International Chief correspondent in wherever the hell...Najef or Mosul or Kandihar"?

No one is our Junior Correspondent in Training, no one is Associate Senior Correspondent Novitiate, no one even just our correspondent. Wolf...don't you choke over these words... "Now to Christianne Candide von Stahl, CNN's chief international and most veteran senior bureau chief in charge of speaking, embedded with our boys in wherever they are." Lucky girl, to be so embedded.

What ever happened to graceful titles like associate correspondent or deputy associate correspondent, or assistant correspondent to the senior correspondent? Why can't Wolf say now to CNN's man (or woman) in Baghdad? Or, to be true to today's jargon, now to CNN's deputy assistant almost senior bureau associate chief. Can everyone truly be senior? If so why say it? Don't we send anyone, excepting our troops fresh from high school or their first jobs, not senior?

Maybe there's work for me. I'm quite senior. No other words would be needed. Now to our senior in Baghdad reporting from his motorized walker as he navigates between embedded senior associate females. Why can't we say a simple with instead of embedded with?

I also wonder…what does it take to be debedded?

A GIRL

FOREWORD

I may get a little soppy as I go through all this and too bad if you don't like it. Also, it's just simple human interest. No impressions, no historical lessons or non-lessons, no questions as to religion or God.

Just a story of a man and a girl 48 years younger. That's all. A girl whose teenage and twenties life would not have been here near me but for my travels to Europe and her family. I felt as all of Gosia's story unfolded as if I were kind of nearer to Poland...that half of my roots. So it was, for me. She gave to me as much as I gave to her - quite a bit as you'll see if you slug your way through all that follows.

Gosia, and Krysia if you too ever read this, please excuse my getting into so much detail.

I just want to tell the whole story. I'd like to tell of the proudest experience of my life, my building with the help of an extraordinary young woman a life that would not have been. There were so many times when I felt I might disappoint you, Gosia, and me at the same time.

So I can explain why I even thought about writing at all. It was your story that started me. Yes I love it and perhaps it's enjoyable to read. No one will tell me which is exactly as it should be. Of course if anyone should publish my travel stories I'll have a better answer. Fat chance. But no matter.

WHO WAS THIS KID?

You'll hear more of Gosia later, in the short 1998 piece describing her home and family in Poznan, Poland. Actually I'd mentioned her before that, as a nine year old kid in 1991, but that 1998 visit was the eye opener. That was the visit of the struggling English, the architecture homework and the explosive piano - the impression of mental focus not to be denied and never before witnessed by me anywhere. This teenager had her act together - what would happen to her? How would she grow?

(Gosia, don't believe any of what I say. You know I'm the king of manip...)

That was her name - Gosia - sounded Go-sha with a very quick "o". Kind of like a Peggy for the English Margaret. Her full name is Malgorzata Maria Magdalena Piechocka. Her family you'll meet as well, in the 1998 piece, her very close sister, her dad and mom.

About a year later in 1999 as I remember they added Deni, an already immense totally beguiling lady Great Dane pup. Her sister Krysia's deepest love and the bane of her dad whose business suits carried drool big time from that day on. Deni as a puppy was, and remained, totally undisciplined, stealing food from everywhere. Marek, the dad, was so ensnared by his now four females that he in a continuing pique refused to bar or gate the kitchen. Deni came to own it. Garbage and dinners ready for the family, everything. Cool, huh? She quickly stood tall enough to clean the tables and also to open high up cabinets. Her stomach, from all the stories told to me, drove her.

Sometime in there a tiny kitten named Kotilka showed up. The photos of this kitten batting away at the ever getting bigger Dane's head are priceless...the kitten smaller than the dog's head. A little while later they adopted a street dog, a gloriously colored Swiss mountain dog cross, whom they named Lusia, so they had over 200 pounds of dogs and an eight pound cat-in-charge.

Marek loved it all - he could go buy more business suits. He truly forced these animals on his family. Why Marek, why?

Gosia as a high school junior achieved good grades in the standard stuff and was gifted with undoubted piano ability. The girls' schooling was a long day of combined required subjects and serious music study. Poland lives a cherished musical backdrop, and not just Chopin. If you've never heard Polish Christmas carols you're missing something otherworldly beautiful.

Especially Stefan Stuligrosz and the Poznan Nightingales, accompanied by organ. I can make you an illegal copy.

I did not particularly target Gosia when I asked if one of the girls might be interested in the exchange student bit. Krysia demurred, Gosia mulled and said yes. I'm certain that Krysia had she come, with her insightfulness, her special warmth, her own soft beauty and her quick brain would have done as well here as her sister. (You too, Krysia, don't believe any of this sweet talk.)

But Krysia had her own immediate future at 18 pretty well planned - two years in Finland were in the offing. Each girl by this time had become a beauty. Life can surprise older people.

So it was that in August of 1999 Gosia showed up at the home of her uncle and grandmother in New York City for me to collect.

What in the world was I, age 66, doing with another teenager? Why did I do this? If she thought she was nervous it was as nothing compared to my own. How to befriend even just temporarily a kid from Poland? I recall we walked the beach and said almost nothing. We drove to Virginia and the best I could do was ask her to read road signs.

Later that summer I even took her to my senior softball games. What could be worse? I just did not want her to be lonely. One night I asked her host parents, of whom I'll speak in a moment, if I might take her to dinner. I did, to an expensive waterfront restaurant here in town; she looking like a model, me feeling like an idiot. I mean what had I gotten myself into?

She stared, I stared, we practiced menu. She knew I was trying and I was already so proud of her for knowing. I had not been so nervous since I myself at 17 dated good looking 17 year olds.

If you consider bringing a foreign student here, on your own, make the student an extraordinary musician, a super student and find a compatibility of religions. St. Mary's High School in Annapolis was wonderful in every way - from Sister Francita, the principal, Rob White the deputy principal, to Vera Mikula the best of all counselors, and all the way through the office staff and student body. Students? The usual; some dull some great. Many a bit in awe of this tall musician so new to this far wealthier American culture. One girl had been asked to kind of host Gosia and she did wonderfully…Christine Kiefer.

Aside from gaining her admission to high school which actually came pretty easily - a so talented Catholic kid and a Catholic high school - I had a tougher job. Mary and I had agreed we would not attempt to parent again and would only be here as needed. So I'd like to recount how I found the family - her so wonderful host family.

THE FERRO FAMILY -
DAN, ANN, FINLEY AND PACKY

I made lots of phone calls. No one wanted to host a foreign student. What's with people? It's only responsibility and money up front. Maybe a world of later love?

I recalled I had run into Ann Ferro, a neighbor, over in the nearby park one day, flying a kite with her young son Packy. Packy from Patrick. Ann, Woodstock veteran that she was, had a very special way about her. Her way of speaking, so personally and gently forcefully, was unique.

I don't think I knew it at the time, but she was the politically appointed head of Maryland's Motor Vehicle Administration. The difference she made was so evident. While she was there customer service was exceptional and after she left it fell apart in a big hurry. I guess this is a stepping stone job but she made some difference. Today, as I write, it's election day here; I can't even find out if the MVA offices are open or not. I'm wrapped all around the voice mail and dumb web site but no answer…Ann would have cured that in the time it takes me to tell you.

So I asked her to possibly check with her friends and all and please get back to me? Very calmly she said to give her a few days. I said of course, what else? She said later I asked if she would host Gosia but I think she was wrong. No matter it was certainly implicit. I was so smooth.

Ann said yes after checking with her family.

I had a kind of fight with Ann a year or so later. She said I was manipulative in working for Gosia, which really frosted me. That she would say it I mean. Of course I was! But coming from a woman who did the state government every day for a living I thought this was a bit much. But we got past that I trust. Right, Ann? You're right I'm right.

I remember that evening for another reason and now I'll get you back...

We had all been in a local pizza joint and Ann's kids made some mention of the servers and cooks. Ann said well of course they're all Italian! Of course, Ann. The fact that they spoke Central American Spanish was... hm...just evidence of language skills. But no, Ann dear, I made no mention of it. Never correct a mom, might not be manipulative but certainly gauche at the least. Nice me, Ann?

Never was this to be told. But why not. Who cares.

And please don't sue me yet. Read more!

The Ferro family was the greatest for Gosia, and she was a new big sister for Finley and Packy. A big sister to learn from and to teach, all of which Dan, Ann and kids did so very well.

More about the Ferros soon. They had strange rules. Like watch the drinking. I mean, give me a break. You'd think since she headed the MVA her family could drink and even drive with impunity. Why in the world might a law enforcement official insist on no drinking while driving?

HIGH SCHOOL - THE FIRST YEAR

St. Mary's High School at the start was no walk in the park. Conversational English was one thing but study at a parochial school was quite another. Vera Mikula, Gosia's advisor, was wise beyond our ease of understanding. The school admitted Gosia as a junior, even though between Poland and the U.S. we had much difficulty in relating curricula.

Vera explained this to us and went on to say that the course load would be light, but not to worry it could be modified. Gosia was upset at first, she wanted more. As it turned out Gosia actually dropped sociology due solely to language. Wise Vera. And I and others helped with her religion studies…religion being heavily philosophical and ecumenical at that level. Or so it seemed to me; obviously I could not help with the study of Catholicism.

In her technical classes that first year, like math and chemistry, Gosia did quite well. Amazingly, with language and all, she even tutored other kids in these subjects. And the school got its first glimpse of an extraordinary pianist. The Ferros continually fought in Gosia's behalf at school; I recall Dan going over and insisting on class changes and coming to complain to me that we needed to do more. You were the best, Dan.

Gosia made the two-hour round trip to Washington many Saturdays that first year, and later the second as

well, to attend a school for Polish kids here in the States.
Diplomat's kids and the like. A bit more stress, but she
sought it out and did it. In case she had to return to Poland
after either high school year she wanted to be up to speed as
best she could.

A few other happenings that first year come to mind.

First, the school musical presentation that spring was,
happily since I love it so much, *Jesus Christ Superstar.* Gosia
carried it instrumentally. The singing and acting overall were
just superb as so many high school plays can be but without
the Polish kid on piano the music would have been canned.
It was all just delicious, as that so wonderful and different
Webber is. I saw it twice of course. My young grandsons as
well.

Now…the first drinking incident. Gosia was all of
17, full boozing age in Poland. Here in Maryland kids that
age have to sneak. We don't know just what she did but she
did come home one night to the Ferros kind of soused. Ann,
the statewide director of don't drink when driving would
have none of that. Gosia was given her warning; once more
and gone. Ah well, I was indeed glad Mary and I were the
unparents, just around the corner. As you'll see, Ann was
indeed serious.

About your English, Gosia. It was already progressing
beautifully. It must help to have a musically retentive mind.
But, as part of your punishment, Ann said less TV. Might
have made total sense with an American kid, but TV for you
was hearing and sounding English. How did you and Ann
work that out? (Your English, now in 2008, is the best except
for those *a's*, *the's* and the *gonna's* to spite me.)

Finally, as you now suspect, one year was not going to be enough for Gosia. Her grades had gotten up to honors levels, she had friends, she had incredible ambition, and she saw opportunity as had so many Poles before her.

I was doomed. What now? What could I do? If she stayed for her senior year here came college. And another host family for that second year? Oh boy.

College? Money? There was none. So I said OK. I was dead meat.

St. Mary's however said no. Big time tears. They said no money for next year and really would not relent. They knew what they had in this kid; she'd become a leader - but they had a problem. They were not, it turned out, fully convinced that her family knew of all this; maybe Gosia and I had pulled a fast one. The semester was about to end and Gosia would stay on, hoping.

Well, Gosia won of course. It was the time of her 18th birthday and her mom was to come from Poland to be with her. I took her mom in to school one morning, to meet teachers and whomever, and Sister Francita, still the principal, took one look at Danuta and said something like I guess there's no doubt you're Gosia's mom and yes, we'd like her to stay for her senior year. No mom and daughter resemblance could have been so clear, face shape and eyes especially. Poor mom, though; Gosia was already almost a head taller. Also we suspect that your drama teacher wanted you, in that she was planning a Gershwin musical.

So that was it. Gosia and I had figured it. The school simply wanted to protect itself. Danuta had come to visit and by serendipity she paved the way for all that would happen -

college followed by a top grad school and great job. Just luck? Who knows.

Earlier that year the most important influence on Gosia's American life came her way. I really don't know how to write this with sufficient feeling and force, and thanks, but I'll try.

Mary Tamplin is her name. Mary headed the Annapolis branch of the Peabody Institute of Johns Hopkins University, usually just referred to as Peabody as is Juilliard in New York City. Peabody, in Baltimore, may or may not have the name recognition Juilliard has but it certainly is one of the finest schools of music in the U.S., both undergraduate and graduate. Mary had two degrees from Peabody.

I had decided with St. Mary's going well that I had to offer to Gosia the piano she loved so much. No big reaction from Gosia. She excelled at it but as events would later show it was not an obsession…no ten hours per day of practice for her. Life was too interesting. With A's in math and science, for example, there was so much to learn and so much to see and experience. Big problem being good at many things.

This girl did in fact tell me more than once that she wished to be the best in the world at something. I had no good answer for her, each time.

Mary Tamplin knew we had money problems, could not afford big time lessons. Still, she auditioned Gosia and took her as a student. I asked of course what about potential?

Mary gave the stock answer...she as a policy never answered such questions. Time would tell. Mary was a very talented sometime performer herself as we would learn but she chose to teach.

Turned out also that Mary had strong Polish roots. But was that the reason she only charged for every second lesson? I doubt it. Maybe one day I'll ask her. She won't answer I'm sure. But can you imagine? Is this the essence of teaching or what?

Gosia, so grateful for all that she had, but with too many things in life to touch, almost cost us Mary a little later. Gosia was not practicing enough. This was not a frivolous thing for Mary; music was her calling. I got wind of it and landed hard on Gosia. A near thing.

What did Mary Rankiewicz Tamplin mean to us? Well, she took Gosia to another level. She prepared Gosia for all her college auditions, ensuring that both the mix of period music and the balance was appropriate. She of course ensured that the performing itself would be top drawer. In effect, it was Mary who got Gosia those three merit scholarships I'll mention later. It was Mary who made Peabody possible for Gosia, her student, four years later.

For Mary just another days's work? I'll never know. I rewarded her by asking if she would take me as a student. I could play; I mean c'mon, I'd played 50 years earlier. What did she say, you think?

Mary...thank you.

THE SENIOR YEAR

More honors, more music - Gosia did the Gershwin play *Crazy for You* - this time. More friends I suppose, the usual. I didn't follow too closely. She was still at the Ferros, gluttons for punishment that they were.

Then…Ann called and said Gosia was being asked to leave her house. Uh oh. Damn. I'd handed this kid-watching problem over to the Ferros I thought. Asked to leave?
Not possible.

Seems the MVA administrator intended to make good on her threat. Gosia still underage had been apprehended along with a few dozen others at a party, with alcohol (heaven and Catholic school forbid) found all about. No hard evidence she'd been drinking as such, but still guilty by however the law reads.

Ann took exactly the right position of course. Woodstock free wheeler or not, she was now THE mom! The example had to be set for Finley and Packy. Never mind that President Bush's daughter was up on a drug charge…they were Republicans. Was it a drug charge? Maybe alcohol?

Second offense and done! Please call your lawyer off now, Ann…ok? What a job you did and what a mom you were, the best.

Still Gosia was about to be a displaced kid. Recall I mentioned Christine Kiefer earlier, as the girl who befriended Gosia right from the start - she and her family stepped in and the housing problem was solved for the moment. It was late in the senior year at least; could have been worse for sure. I envisioned a big-time problem when Ann called but thank you Kiefers. Very much.

A little later Gosia came to live with Mary and me, until college, and we who wanted no parenting loved it. She had to do a paper for the court admitting that she was a bad girl indeed which she did although she was not (I hope).

That was pretty much it for the senior year. More honors and college plans. College? Right. How? Who was to pay? I could offer no real help.

College for sure. It was to be. Gosia told me. Together we would find the money. Gosia did by the way work every part-time job she could from baby sitting to teaching piano, tutoring and even hostessing in a local restaurant. But it was one dicey time, for maybe three months and well into summer.

Admission was no problem. Applications, essays, music auditions, and then admittance to all four she selected. But each cost some $25,000 per year and Gosia as a non citizen was not eligible for any governmental assistance. All her friends were in and making plans and she, a terrific student with so much to offer, again hung in limbo. Into July.

I'd like to say thanks, in its turn now, to Towson University and especially to a lady who matched students to scholarships in the music department - Mary Ann Criss. Towson had initially committed to about $10,000 in merit awards but after my 547th badgering call Mary Ann asked if another $5,000 would help. I jumped, I had already decided so in my mind. We were short but would risk it. You, Mary Ann, joined the growing list of those we owe so much.

Gosia…how did it feel when I called you?

And, as it happened, Towson's super music department was instrumental in everything good that was

to happen. We again were lucky…Towson, Baltimore, the
Nielsens, Peabody to come.

THE COLLEGE YEARS

The first college year is perhaps the most formative
year in growing up. Away from the shelter of home. In this
case quite a far distance away. With all of us lucky Americans
we, of course, come home a year later knowing all the
answers to life's deepest questions. I mean all. For Gosia I'm
not sure. Maybe she still had a question or two.

Dorm roommates were bestowed and a bit off the wall
as far as she was concerned. She was too probably, for them.
All the usual budgeting and feeding oneself, now on her own.
A problem was that she was placed in the international dorm,
with hardly any useful spoken English. I puzzled at this policy.
The Ferros and I each gave some spending money which of
course helped; and Towson University was not for wealthy
kids, but still.

She'd taken the English tests required for admission
and done well enough but I was still concerned. College can
be a bit intimidating even with super language skills and
Gosia was not nearly there yet. I had a kind of connection
though, and you, Clarinda, stepped in and really put my
mind at ease. Clarinda Harriss was a personal friend, a very
special personality and talent herself, a poet, and by chance
headed Towson's English department. Clarinda guided Gosia
to the appropriate English classes and I knew with Clarinda
watching I could relax a bit.

We had known that this smallish close-to-Baltimore
university, formerly a teacher's college of no great renown,

had a music department with at least one or two names. But as time passed we saw that we had truly gotten lucky. Gosia did indeed major in piano performance - it was her strength and staying with strength often makes sense - and Towson came through. Two professors at Towson became her pillars...Eva Mengelkoch, Gosia's teacher and a little later a strong Baltimore music force and Reynaldo Reyes, not her own teacher but a powerful presence.

Living got better with each semester, as did roommates, grades were Dean's List from the start, a half dozen or so jobs were worked for spending money and college rolled along. This young woman, now, did not flag in her focus...no way.

Two major and continuing events dominated the middle college years...a horrible car accident and the coming to the states of Gosia's parents.

Her parents could not just sit home in Poland, doing well enough I supposed from what I knew, but so concerned that they were not helping their daughter at her American college as much as they might. Krysia was living with her boyfriend in Finland, looking carefully at a life there, but Gosia was kind of exposed. No one but maybe me was watching her.

Marek and Danuta, dad and mom, decided separately, I forget who first, to come here and work. Marek had his brother and mother in New York City, and a place to live. But he was also looking hard at several different jobs in his own country, hoping to build a long term job situation.

Danuta was as usual terribly busy with her own music, her teaching. What might she do here? You don't just acquire a constituency of parents calling out to you to teach their kids music overnight. At home, in Poznan, she was in high demand; she taught not just piano, but violin, guitar, voice and even choir. But here no one knew her.

She decided, this educated woman, as had so many before her to swallow pride and offer to provide elder care if I might find her something here close to Gosia. It's so easy to say this, for me now. She would be a caregiver. But I still wonder how many American women might do this…give up a professional career to house sit or baby sit. I suppose this is unfair of me; I suppose many would. I'd better let this one go.

I did indeed find her something. Another wonderful family came into Gosia's life, a family who now, in very late 2008, are still in her life. In fact she lives with them now as she studies at Peabody.

I mean a spectacular family. Meet Karl and Elisabeth Nielsen of Timonium, Maryland, just a few miles from Gosia at Towson University. Karl and I had gotten in touch in that they needed some help in their own family. A close relative was very sick, and Elisabeth needed help in giving their beautiful home the tender loving care that she, Elisabeth, might otherwise manage. Also, after meeting Karl it was clear this was a special chance to make new friends. They also were very devout and giving people, and had shared their home with another young Polish woman just before.

Karl took my word for this new Polish family being so talented and good, and he called Elisabeth then in Europe visiting her own elderly parents. We all agreed. He offered also to help Danuta find students here, something that never worked out because of the need for her to be a family caregiver. Teaching income, we hoped, would lessen the need for him to help with Gosia's college.

This very intimate shared family experience lasted six months for Danuta, as long as allowed by visa. During this time she and Elisabeth became friends, and Gosia came to know Karl, Elisabeth and their four sons. Gosia as I write lives with Karl and Elisabeth saving the expense of her own apartment; and unless I miss my guess may be the daughter they never had. I've only asked Karl two or three times - the answer, very brief, would come back don't worry we'll keep her.

I'd been replaced! I'd done myself pretty much out of a job.

No tears. It had to be...and we got so lucky with Karl and Elisabeth. You guys...continue to enjoy this new daughter if she be that.

(I must note that Nielsen is a fictitious name. The real family is so wonderful they might not wish my invading their privacy.)

Marek, her dad, did in fact also spend quite a bit of time here, doing whatever he did to help his brother, and made a very substantial contribution to ongoing college expense. My own role at this point was no longer to watch every nickel; Gosia was on top of it all and her family had come over to help. And help they did, as tough as it must have been.

This may all sound like the usual college story, but remember Gosia was not eligible for student loans, her parents lived 4,000 miles away, and we had to come up with some $25,000 per year. It was not the usual story. Not by a mile.

The accident? I'm not going to say too much about it. I'd been terribly concerned about health insurance from day one of Gosia's arrival a few years before. She had very slim coverage in high school. But, thank heaven, she now had the usual good university insurance.

A friend's car, she as a passenger in the back seat, was broadsided. Another friend next to her was critically injured, from head down to her legs. For some reason of physics I don't quite understand - the car impacted Gosia's side - Gosia escaped with but major bruises. My own daughter, Diane, who with her family lived close to Gosia, was first to be with her. I told you, Di, you were great that day and even later as you kept in touch. Gosia became a friend of that family as well, baby sitting and once or twice a music lesson for my two grandsons.

The medical bill was over $4500. Yea university-provided insurance. She had stitches on her head, a bruised back, and a beat-up wrist frightening her as a pianist, wrist therapy forever, but all this healed. Enough on this subject.

Gosia kept her own counsel on many things and especially with her social life. Fine. None of my business for sure. But one time, as it happened when her mom was here, Gosia wanted us to meet some guy. So we did. Bjorn the Swede. Bjorn the Magnificent.

Yeah, a good looking guy. But never, I mean never, had I met someone so ordinary so stuck on himself. He was eloquent in his own behalf. A cell phone salesman just finishing college. This guy may now be king of some cell company and a multimillionaire, but what a jerk. You, Gosia, asked me recently why I never said anything to you

at the time. Right. You would have killed me. I know it
might have hurt a little at the end, but as it was you were
so kind to this fool. Anything beyond the first one hour was
too much of you for him. I say this knowing others said
good things about him then. Ah well.

And of course I'd endeared myself super big time
to your sister once or twice by answering questions about
guys. Once the fault of your mom and once asked directly
by your sister. You three are a pain sometimes. Big surprise,
women a pain.

Your junior and senior year piano recitals were a treat
for so many of us. Yes, we all knew you had no intention of
performing. But, like it or not, you were good...very good.
Imagine if you really cared enough to perform. I forget the
programs but the highlight of course was you doing *Rhapsody
in Blue* your senior year. A simple little piece. Your mom made
it for the junior recital and your dad and New York family for
the senior. Marek, apologies for getting on your case about
the camera. I should have been more understanding.

JOBS AND GRADUATE SCHOOL

So you graduated. Dean's List all the way.

It was Peabody you were after and you were accepted
pretty quickly. This one was even more expensive; what was
it - $40,000 per year? You and I knew that you'd have to
go into stalling mode after acceptance while the money got
sorted out. Peabody gave very little fellowship or scholarship

help to first year students and you were not one of the lucky few. This is a very top rank graduate school.

You signaled acceptance, as I recall, and we thought and thought about this. I know you went kind of nuts turning over ideas in your own mind. But you'd apparently impressed your particular degree program head in your interviews and he said, informally, that if you wanted to work and wait a year you would still have a spot. It would require re-application but you'd be in the following year.

Gosia's major by the way was not performance but something vaguely described, to me, as the science of music and audio technology. Very demanding physics and electronics, nothing she'd had, but she had the special advantage of being a trained and skilled pianist. She also had an unusually fine and discriminating ear for sound and notes, which was of special benefit in this program.

As I write you are reconsidering majors. But you had the money solution.

Gosia had the ok to work for a year on her visa so work it was and save bucks. This she did and began at Peabody the following year. She tells me she is the only female in one class of 20 males. Gee, what a problem.

Also, she mentioned that one teacher seemed to be calling on her too often with do you know stuff. She quickly became annoyed, she told me. Soooo, with a grin, she said she got him. She began to purposely ask lots of questions and he quickly got the message and stopped bugging her. I wish I'd thought of that myself in graduate school, instead of sitting dumb and dull.

I guess I've now told it all about college. She did it and more, and is on her way to who knows what but she will excel in lights somewhere as I said before.

Jobs? Well, first of all she was restricted to work in her field under the conditions of the student visa. This meant the arts or something very close to the arts. Not an easy field in which to find work. I helped craft the visa request to keep it as broad as possible. She found such work and is now the Executive Assistant and Operations Manager for the Maryland Humanities Council. She also managed an internship at the Baltimore Symphony Orchestra.

The Council, thanks Steve and Peggy, arranged for her work visa, relieving her of the pressure of the student visa, and in effect giving her six years to push on toward the green card. The Council? We'll see. One promotion so far.

Pretty much the end of this story. Of what I have to say. Of what she's done, this kid now young woman from Poland .

THE FUTURE

Try and hang on. We'll see. I say this to myself, I gotta hang on. I truly do expect to see your name in lights somewhere. So please GG speed it up a bit? Don't worry too much about what and where.

You're my only hope. You asked once will I do this again. No way. You were much too much trouble for me. Thanks for coming, Gosia Girl.

*Mountain
tips on the
Czech border*

*Gosia
and the
author*

Gosia (left) and her sister Krysia after Gosia's high school graduation

Gosia in her twenties

Lucy the mountain dog and Deni

Kotilka disciplining Deni the Great Dane

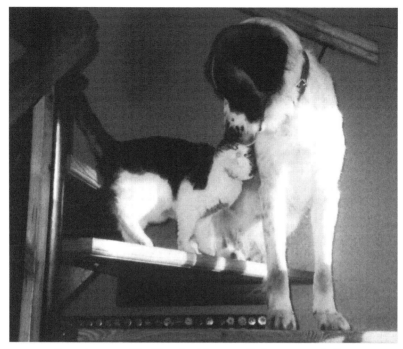

Love between Kotilka the kitten and the mountain dog

Lucy taking a break from the action

EUROPE

FOREWORD

I began to write in the summer of 2006 with the Mideast once again in flames, as Hezbollah in Lebanon attacked and Israel retaliated big time. The world wondered if finally one or more cities or nations will be destroyed. What truly is the difference between impressions and thousands of years of documented history? We twist each and act on each. It would be nice if someone could explain why a 30 second take can be the equivalent of hundreds of years of study. And, for me, how God can have so many faces as to confuse a reasoning thinker.

So I try to craft impressions of travel things that happened to me, quite different from the new reality of the real Pamplona and Texas and even CNN as well - all in earlier parts of this book.

As I say a number of times, these travel tales are told as impressions. I saw and felt as I traveled. Here I tell these stories as I remember my emotions at the time. For someone most often so detached and unemotional, I did get caught up.

Hope you enjoy the humor and irony, and especially the people, I found in so many places. If I've made a mistake, hardly a probability with my memory, please forgive me. I took no notes on any of my trips.

A WORD ON GERMANY AND POLAND

The travel experiences I chronicle here are for the most part stories of fun and good people. Some are of things I definitely should not have done, but did. Some are even embarrassing. But all left impressions and the international world of travel is made more of impressions than deep thought.

Germany? Poland? You wonder about the countries involved, primarily Germany and Poland, and with just a touch of France and others? Why not Greece, Italy - places about which everyone writes? Sorry, no apology.

This was the way it unfolded; the experiences and events happened as they happened - with so many wonderful things coming my way in, of all places, Germany and Poland. Beautiful, storied lands if history matters to you.

Germany was and is central to momentous happenings in Europe. Other nations may argue the present, but when thought of in context of the full 20th century, there is no argument. Still thought of as a nation of crude stereotypes, it is in truth, as I write, not that at all. It has become a multi-cultural, thoroughly introspective and self-doubting nation with an aging and shrinking population. Although still a nation of order and of profound technical skills, Germany now must compete on all fronts for acceptance and for the future of its narrowed youthful base.

It does all this with an awareness of its past that is, still now, a paranoia, and yet with a gentle energy that makes me wonder how such terrible cross currents can be lived at all. There was even a national doubt about all the German flags displayed during the 2006 soccer world cup. Imagine any other nation reticent about showing its own flag.

A likeable nation it may never be. A lighthearted Italy it will never be. Germany is serious. And still Germany is loaded with graceful, gentle, helpful people. Traveling in Germany is a joy, and if one is awake and alert...the food is fine.

Poles and Germans have not been best friends. The border changed every ten minutes for some 200 years, with the Poles usually the losers except when major wars and imposed settlements bailed them out. The initial attack on Poland that officially began WW II was the shelling by a German battle cruiser of the formerly German city of Danzig on the Baltic. Now it is Gdansk, given to the Poles at the end of WW I so that the Poles might have an outlet to the sea. Almost all of Northern Poland was either Pomerania or East Prussia for centuries, very German.

But now the two nations are members of the European Union and of NATO. They travel freely, one to the other. They see a common interest in trade and while differences remain, especially in income levels and in population makeup and religious influence. They are, amazingly, living a partnership many would deem a political miracle.

So what is Poland today? It is a nation bursting at the seams with ambition but still frozen by conservative, even reactionary, forces in everyday life. What do young Poles say to this? They said this...over one million mostly young Poles have already emigrated to find work only one short year after Union membership. Older Poland had better get the message; change or wither. Those are the only long term choices, despite the progress I note next. (In 2008, as I prepare this for publication, young Poles are returning in droves.)

In the 17 years since my first visit the nation had come alive and the pace of openness and westernizing is accelerating Markets are buzzing, roads are so much improved but not enough so, incomes remain low but opportunities are improved, and most important many more Poles now smile. If Poland may offer just a bit more to its young people as I said, and soon - especially more freedom to study with an eye to careers not impacted by the Polish past - the sky will be the limit as to what Poland may accomplish in the Europe of the early 21st century. There is an economic power base waiting to be filled, as other nations experience aging and other problems. Certainly stronger economic ties to Germany should be explored.

Travel in Poland, as you'll see, is very exciting. Especially on the roads. And, if you care about recent history, as fulfilling as any travel can be. Very, very emotionally challenging as well. Food? Enjoy the eastern Europe specialities. Every good sized town or city I've visited has newer restaurants, and many of course of the old eastern European world also, that are as good as any here in the states. Not too many of five star rating, but so what. Ask questions and order sensibly.

I will tell you...Polish breads and rolls are the best by far of any I've ever had anywhere. And fresh by necessity, harvest and bake and consume, the only way possible in a country never, in its past, wasting one piece of fresh bread. Give it a go, you'll see what I mean.

So…you might like some colorful travels? I hope my stories will give you pleasure.

1971 - MY FIRST VISIT TO EUROPE AND A DANGEROUS NEAR MISS

I was an employee of the U.S. Department of Defense, being sent to West Germany to discuss NATO issues. Years earlier, my new wife and I had turned down a chance to live in West Germany, when as a young officer in the U.S. Army my guided missile speciality made me a prime candidate. Looking back I think we both regret that decision; it would have been a wondrous thing for a young couple to be given this expenses paid excuse to travel all through Europe. So in 1971, with my roots and my curiosity about all things in any way tieing to 20th century European events, I finally made my first trip.

The meetings were nothing as I recall, breaking bread and drinking great beer with many military and civilian officials nearby to Frankfurt, deep in the U.S. occupation sector. A good number of my colleagues were back and forth between the U.S. and Germany continually, as the west and the Soviet Union sparred in these most bitter days of the cold war. They had had their travel opportunities! As the meetings wound down, a thought crossed my mind; why not pop up to Berlin, take my shot at something a little special?

This most complex and infamous of German cities was then split between the four occupying powers…the U.S., the Soviet Union, France and England. It was a hot bed of intrigue and espionage, with all sides, including both

Germanies, actively spying and recruiting spies. There were undoubtedly dozens of double agents, so much so that it was a virtual guarantee that anything of any cold war value said or done would be known to everyone in a matter of days. Disinformation was the name of the game; all sorts of military, political, economic and personal information was spread around. Most of this took place in the western sectors because of the relative easy of entry. The Soviets and their East German buddies only welcomed visitors with deutschmarks or dollars. And all visitors to the East were shadowed by one police official or another, making it a real fun place to be.

Even getting to West Berlin wasn't easy. You could only fly in one of the three air corridors allowed by agreement with the East Germans. The southern route, originating east of Frankfurt, was mostly used by U.S. aircraft. The central and northern routes were used primarily by British and French planes. All flights had to stay below 10,000 feet allegedly for reasons of pressurization but in truth because they might be watched and harassed more easily

Communist fighters patrolled these air corridors with exuberance, and incidents and near accidents were commonplace. Talk about exciting air travel. Contrast this with air travel in Europe now, with dozens of airlines crisscrossing Germany at any given moment. You could drive in of course, but the autobahns across East Germany were a pain then and watched very carefully. This was the German Democratic Republic, we must remember. (It isn't just in the current mid east that the word "democracy" has mysterious meanings.)

Berlin had three or four airports in various stages
of building; Tegel in the French sector, Tempelhof in the
American, Schonefeld in the Soviet and Gatow in the
British. Tegel actually was built during the blockade, by the
French with help from some 17,000 West Berliners! From
Frankfurt it was Tempelhof, delightfully deposited inside a
clotch of high rise apartment buildings. Tempelhof also had
a nearby 400 foot chimney, quite close to the flight path and
something best avoided. A rundown on the airlift and what
it accomplished is a bit beyond this story, but let it be said
that it was one of the greatest, riskiest and most appreciated
humanitarian gestures in human history - a free city was kept
alive, kept reasonably healthy and kept from Communist
tyranny.

We were flying lots of 727's then, a funny looking
very tail-heavy aircraft with an early record of plopping
down short of runways as pilots tried to keep the tail up. So
imagine our joy when the pilot announced...well, the weather
is rough and we're going in very fast, with a steep descent
just over that last ringing apartment building. Imagine as you
approach any big time U.S. airport being told well...er...
we'll try it but no guarantees. You might be asking yourself if
a job without travel could be a little sweeter.

Bump, bump, whoosh...we were down. No problem.
I was in the capital of WWII Germany, the home of Hitler,
Goering, Himmler and their pals.

To be in Berlin is to wonder why about a zillion
things. Even in half rebuilt 1971, but especially before the
war, Berlin was a city of a mystery composite culture. It
was wonderful music and literature, education, and fine
schools and colleges. It had been the city of von Karajan and
many writers, of Cabaret, of elegant Charlottenburg and

the intrigue of the Hotel Adlon, of Prussian eagles and the infamous Hitler bunker, of Kennedy's "Ich bin ein Berliner", and of innumerable parks and lakes. Before the war it was also unfathomally brutal, unless of course one could fathom Nazism. In 1971 it was still brutal, both in the East and West, but somewhat less showy in its culture. The West of course very proudly showed its new prosperity, with music, stores and restaurants and theater; while the East displayed the face of mindlessness, of unrepaired war damage, of near poverty, of terrible fear and of no reason to be there but for compulsion.

So, of course, I decided to have a look at the east. Dumb me.

At that time I was carrying a top secret clearance from the U.S. government. This was not uncommon. Many who worked in defense matters were investigated and then processed for such clearance. It was as high a security clearance as one could get, but for certain closely held nuclear and policy clearances.

We who wished to go to the East sector boarded a bus, as I recall at Checkpoint Charlie, and then slipped easily out of the U.S. zone. I had with me my tourist passport, in that my official passport, which I had used otherwise for my journey, would be of no use. The U.S. had no diplomatic relations with the German Democratic Republic, the GDR, and official visits simply did not happen. In short, I was entering the Soviet, or GDR, zone, masquerading as a civilian tourist, and entering a most unfriendly and belligerent nation. The East Germans wanted hard currency, and maybe an occasional defector, but otherwise

we were about as welcome as President W would be in
Iran or Lebanon as I write. Quite unwelcome indeed. I of
course had entered quite surreptitiously, carrying with me,
in my mind, whatever secrets I had from years of work in
the Pentagon.

So I was a bit nervous. More than a bit. But it was
a little late. I was entering East Germany, the happy land
of the Stasi, the KGB-like East German secret police, and
disappearing westerners. At that time I had a wife and three
children 12 and under.

No one knew I was where I was.

Our bus, an ancient version of a village school bus, was
stopped immediately on entering the Soviet zone. There were
perhaps 20 of us, happily in pursuit of a glimpse of one of the
most depressing cities on earth. A woman in uniform climbed
aboard, an East German VOPO or border patrol person.
Armed, of course.

She was, sadly, the most unattractive human I had
ever laid eyes on. About five feet tall, she was some 180
muscular pounds. Square face, square shoulders, broad nose
and mouth and small, very small gray eyes. All of this set off
by this horrible uniform, something also in gray with gray
hat, and as I remember service ribbons of some kind. I recall
thinking…what kind of ribbons does a border policeman
earn?

This fearsome creature, representing tyranny and
silence, stopped directly in front of each tourist and stared
for some five minutes. It seemed longer. Was it five minutes
each? It seemed like a half hour. She pretended to compare

our passport picture with each face. But surely that was a ruse; who would be dumb enough to fake a tourist passport with someone else's face? There were easier ways of sneaking into the East zone at that time. Agents could pass almost freely, by prearrangement.

So what was she after? Some dummy like me? This particular dummy?

She handed my passport back to me and moved on. When she had finished and debarked, the bus started up and continued on for a short while through those virtually empty and so colorless streets. It parked in front of a small store, what we would call now a convenience store, but so terribly bare, and we all got the standard speech on what we could and could not do (no pictures of course), how far we might wander, how to shop (a bad joke) and when we had to be back. The shopping? My recollection is that there were no other shops, certainly none that would draw one's eye. Imagine the contrast between a Times Square and a huge parking lot amid bombed out shells. That was what we had in the difference between West and East Berlin.

I had by no means gotten over my being-stared-at session with the muscular lady VOPO. I continued to think what the hell am I doing here? And, of course, I couldn't just sit on the bus; that would be to really invite trouble. So I pushed myself to get up and out, and go walking. I dared not even look behind me, for the tail that followed almost everyone in East Berlin according to those who knew. I faked interest in seeing things for a few blocks, bought something trivial as part of my show of good tourist, and re-boarded the bus before anyone else had returned. I waited for maybe an hour and we left.

I thought years later, had PCs existed then and she had loaded a Pentagon telephone directory, available to anyone at that time, I would have been matched up with my job, grabbed, and quite possibly simply disappeared. Remember, I was traveling as a tourist and tourists did disappear - especially those in sensitive jobs masquerading as tourists. Spying I think it was called.

Bye, bye…disappeared to the Gulag. Or just gone. So long family. That was an extremely stupid thing for me to do.

LONDON, BRUSSELS AND PARIS - 1974; FOUR FLEETING DAYS AND ONLY FIGHTER PLANES

Only my second visit to Europe, this was not notable - business meetings in all three cities. I know I'm writing but truth is truth. We were doing a report on the major NATO nations Germany, the UK and France, had to press some flesh. All that come to mind were the wonderful air force social club in London, a holdover from WW II for sure in that it was totally Brit on the distaff side, my colleague turning his ankle and almost breaking it in a hidden anti-American street grate in Paris, and my seeing in my mind's eye dozens of those WW I biplanes doing combat wheelies over the Channel as we crossed.

But all, however so trivial and passing at the time, were imperceptibly becoming a piece of the store of feeling to see so much more Europe and do so much more that was building in me.

Zoom and gone. No impressions from this one. Hang in there.

Brussels, Bruges and London - 1977;
Food Prepared Finnishly

Mary and I flew to Brussels; another NATO trip for me. Brussels was and still is NATO's headquarters city. More silly but seemingly essential at the time conferences. (I had served as one of the key war gamers and it was very much still a time of preparing for the Soviet attack on Europe. In fact, in one of my computerized sets of runs I had Brussels overrun in three days any which way I tried to play it short of nuclear. So this was pretty big stuff back then.)

Mary did a ton of touring during my meetings and maybe she should write this piece on Brussels. But let it be said by me that never before and not since have I been served mussels like those of 1977 Brussels - North Sea moules mariniere or with white wine - huge platters of just the right sized, sweet and lightly garliced, super-sized, moules. As we all know, mussels are not expensive but can be tiny and often not worth the time, despite the price, to even open the shell. (We very recently experienced this silliness in an expensive French restaurant.) But I say go and try Brussels. First excuse I get, I'm back there. We did it blindly I might add, an ordinary tourist joint.

Bruges, on the coast, with its beautiful streets and canals was but a short train ride. Definitely a worthwhile side jaunt. Most notably, the Bruges geese didn't like us. We were charged and spat at innumerable times. They may have had early warning of George W. Bush. Or maybe, back in 1977, they were Gaullist geese on travel.

We checked out London on the way back. I slept a bit, she toured and walked and rode the No. 28 bus everywhere. She also got very tight with an 83 year old doorman. I had far more problem with certain of the London accents than I did speaking English and getting along on the continent. But London, without my going into any detail, is certainly a must to visit. Great people, great timeless things to see.

Food? Right up there with Finland, I recently read somewhere. I imagine this is unfair to one or the other. Just a temporally unbalanced and actually totally silly impression. I've never had Finnish food prepared Finnishly.

London, now in 2008, has an impressive rundown of highly rated restaurants. Time to go back.

France and Iceland 1982 - MAD, U.S. Military Planning and a Wood Carving that Made Up for Everything

I was still more or less employed within the U.S. defense community. Back then this was not something to be embarrassed about or ashamed of in the slightest. We all knew who the "enemy" was, and we, the United States of America, had some good friends throughout the world. My nation had played a leading role in stopping fascism, in rebuilding Europe, and in stalemating communist thoughts of expansion.

The U.S. had friends? You doubt this? Read your 20th century history.

It was an extraordinarily dangerous time, with MAD ruling the day. For those who may not know this so attractive acronym, it stood for "mutually assured destruction". We and the Soviets were reasonably assured of being able to totally destroy the other, and the world, if either side started serious trouble. In fact, the real danger was accident or miscalculation, as in the 1960's Cuban missile crisis. The fact that the world escaped destruction, looking back, is tribute only to man's ability to muddle though; certainly not to his wisdom. Perhaps today, with nuclear weapons and hatred spreading the world over, a combination I suspect even God has not prepared for, we may pray for more good luck.

Please forgive my occasional references to God. I really don't know why I do this, in that I have no use for organized religion. In truth, there are some who would argue that organized religion, of the sort I describe next, can easily be shown to be the worst calamity to ever befall mankind.

I think these call-outs to God are possibly because I feel so helpless, even in just telling of my travels, and so worried about my grandchildren, that I must appeal to someone somewhere. As a dear friend, a devout Catholic, recently said to me, there is quite a difference between faith and religion. The kinds of religions that feel compelled to export themselves, that collect big bucks money, that find ways to sponsor killing, that require obeisance…these I despise. Quiet faith and a belief in some rational order; these are things that are indeed good. I suppose in mentioning God perhaps I seek. I'm truly certain man alone given enough time will destroy everything unless Someone intervenes.

Back to travel, a simpler subject.

In 1982, Iceland called. (Did it not call you?) It was, after all, a key outpost in NATO's defense of western Europe. It stood astride sea and air lanes to the U.S. and as such was key to both re-supply of Europe and detection of Soviet submarines that might threaten both the United Kingdom and the U.S. So…I was asked to visit and to comment on the adequacy of NATO's and Icelandic defenses.

The U.S. had committed to Iceland's defense a U.S. Army reserve tank company.

Think about this for a moment. The island was generally volcanic, glacial and quite difficult to transit, geographically exposed, vulnerable to air and sea attack, and in the political world that defined the day absolutely essential to NATO. So, what do we, the U.S. do? We propose to defend the island with an under-equipped, outmoded, far distant, tank unit, maybe some 30 or so WW1l tanks hanging about in Kansas or somewhere. Great military minds. Old frozen-up tanks transiting glaciers while island bases were destroyed by air and sea forces. My boss, John Brinkerhoff, a very creative and senior Pentagon official, knew what a joke this was.

Clearly this cried out for one of our best and brightest to check into. But I was sent. I guess the others were not available. We proposed to do what we could.

Perhaps not everyone realizes this but Paris lies on the direct route from Washington's Dulles airport to Keflavik, the airport and NATO base right next to Reykjavik, Iceland. At least it does if you fly with government money, with assistance from Pentagon travel experts, and can call up a dense fog over Iceland requiring a diverted flight. We had all that going for us. A better planned trip I'd never taken. Sorry, taxpayer, but we had to detour...to Paris. Bitter pill.

I had with me a close colleague and friend. I'd invited him in that he'd taken me to Hawaii several times on business and that clearly qualified him, otherwise knowing zilch of NATO, to help in checking out Iceland. This was the way in the U.S. Defense Department then. Of course it differs so greatly now. Boondocks are unknown now.

Thus it was Michael Farmer and I found ourselves stranded in Paris, not in cooler and somewhat less enticing November Reykjavik. We had to adjust. I mean - Paris in 1982 - how did one get by? We had to fill time waiting for Iceland to open up and a call to our flight.

Paris. What to do? A terrible problem. Well, I did have friends, a thought that had not really ever left my mind even back when scheming my trip with the Pentagon folks. Maybe if we were "forced" to divert I might find someone to feed us.

So I called Isabelle Sauzay, a young woman of 20 or so who had been an exchange student with us a few years back. She and her then boyfriend Ivano Ballerini had both spent time with us.

Isabelle was petite, maybe 5'1", very pretty and not exactly short of youthful French personality and opinion. Every third word was merde, sometimes actually used in context. Far more often it was just used. Ivano was then a basketball player and already a coach of one of the premier

French women's teams. He was best remembered by my wife for parading around one of our local best-keep-all-covered beaches, at age 18, in little more than a jock. Great build, strong Greek God legs and that jock only.

Isabelle and Ivano rendezvoused with us almost immediately and we were saved from having to play alone in Paris. Michael, poor untraveled sort that he was, huge eyes and bald but for long side hair and a beard, and wearing a floppy cape-like rain coat, had been stared at on our few walks alone, apparently mistaken for a kind of American Jesus. He had been getting nervous. Our French guides were welcome.

A night or two later we were at Ivano's parents' house for dinner. His family was Italian French, and quite possibly very communist. I suspected so at any rate. His father, Gilberto, spoke no English, and his mother stayed most of the evening in the kitchen passing out to us course after course of the most incredible seafoods and pastas. The languages spoken around the table were French, Italian, Friulian (from the Friuli region of eastern Italy) and English. Almost every sentence went through a couple of translations.

Michael stayed out of it if pretty much. Ivano's baby sister, a five year old absolute doll named Letizia, found Michael compelling and spent most of her evening on his lap staring and touching his beard and strange side hair. He had no children, and he was fascinated by this little girl. Meantime, as the dishes, with their sauces, got richer and richer the wines got darker and darker and omigod more and more potent. Slowly but most definitely I got not drunk but totally soused. Gilberto and I, as the seniors, sat side by side. We had no common language and could not converse but by the 18th bottle or so had our arms around one another. We were new buddies, the American defense official and the Italo French communist. Loopy buddies.

But, with it all, Gilberto had to show us his collection of wood carvings out in the garage. Isabelle and Ivano accompanied us, which I welcomed. Ivano was strong and I was polluted. But what was the big deal about wood carvings?

I recall only one. It was a sculpted, quite detailed wood carving of masculine magnificence complete with two wooden plums at the back end, about 15 inches in all, corked and fillable from the back. A device for wine tasting. Isabelle, however French and all, had the good grace to blush.

After we slept it all off, kind of, Michael and I went on to Iceland. Gilberto, very sadly, died of a rampaging cancer just six months later and the friend I had made was gone to me and his family.

Iceland, incidentally, was not kind to me. I had not slept it off. I spent the better part of three days hung over the toilet one way or another while Michael flew about seeing everything this beautiful island has to offer and even seeing Soviet aircraft up close.

Israel, Paris, Frankfurt and London - 1988; Always Bring Chinese Spare Ribs

A strange set of stops and events.

The idea at the time was to visit Israel and check on business possibilities. I had never been there and certainly it was worth seeing. Unbelievably, in context of today's world, it was even fairly quiet. No Intifada even. Guns in plain view everywhere nonetheless. I recall one quick happening: I was riding the bus from Tel Aviv to Jerusalem, sitting next to young soldier, a guy maybe twenty at best. A boy. In uniform and with his rifle between his legs…as he slept. I tried a little conversation, but no luck. He slept, deeply. Sleeping on a commuter bus with your automatic rifle loaded and between your knees.

This was not your basic commuter bus in New York or Paris. This was not a world I knew at all.

Although a business friend, who had invited me to Israel specifically to make potential business contacts, did in fact introduce me to some 25 people over the course of a week nothing ever came to us in the way of continuing business. These new contacts ranged all the way from a Stalingrad survivor who wanted to export buttons to the U.S. to a young army major with a .45 caliber pistol in his briefcase. The major joined me in an empty dining room, sat with his back to a wall so he might see everything and even posted his sergeant near the entrance. He did admit to being somewhere in the Israeli intelligence community, and was of necessity always on his guard. Particularly when doing business.

Having no idea where to stay in Tel Aviv I had put myself at a small, turned out to be kosher, tourist hotel. It was probably me, since back then I passionately loved spare ribs, all things beefy including hot dogs, and hated cheeses of all kinds, but the food was just awful. Except for one meal at that friend's house where I made the acquaintance of fish eyes as an appetizer - the rest of the meal was wonderful - I had not one decent meal that week. I was in full stomach revolt by my last night. I knew both Arabs and Jews ate pork, but could not find any place to get my beloved ribs. Or anything decent by my spoiled American standards.

Another very strong impression was the noise level whenever people met. Never had I been anywhere near so many people arguing, literally screaming, at each other. I wonder if this continues to this day, in wartime? The tourists were the most pleasant people on the streets, something that just amazed me.

We were quite late departing Tel Aviv and very late arriving Frankfurt, much too much so for my connecting flight to London. So…and so sadly…Lufthansa put me up at a five-star hotel.

The next morning I ate every sausage known to man, about ten times over. And then flew on to Paris, where that flight was also missed necessitating another stop over and finding a later flight to London. A shame, but another accidental stop in Paris.

Again, wonderful Isabelle Sauzay came to rescue me. Always, since she had been our French daughter as the exchange student, Isabelle was there for us even if it were years between visits. Now she was 29 years old, and so incredibly French - down to her delicious so rich accent when speaking English.

Isabelle was very close to her fathers's mother, her paternal grandmother. Her dad had died years before, and this was her connection to that side of her family. And so it was that I came to visit for lunch her grandmother's picture-book beautiful apartment in Paris.

I should mention that the night before, after arrival from Frankfurt and the five-star feed stop, had been exactly what one should expect…miserable. Those 45 sausages and bacons, eggs, juices, fine coffee and what all had not taken to living comfortably in my gut. Not at all. Isabelle's so pretty apartment was tiny, with the toilet almost in full view and certainly full earshot. She said… "noise, what noise?" Sweet girl. Had my stomach not itself kept me awake assuredly my own noises would have.

Still, off I went for a modest…right…French lunch in an elegant home.

I don't recall how many wines, all red this time, or how many courses, but it was truly elegant and Isabelle and her grandmom were gracious beyond belief. I survived, or so I thought.

Zip…off to London for my flight to the U.S. Heathrow. I checked in, waited an hour or so and boarded the plane. The last I remembered was walking down the aisle.

Consciousness returned in a local hospital. I was told I simply passed out, twitched a bit, and was carted off having provided a thrill for the nearby passengers. The wonderful Brit nurse told me all was well and I could leave. They found no problems. I figured yeah right socialized medicine and please do go home. Probably needless to say, I was a bit scared.

On returning to the U.S. I did in fact have every possible test. No evidence of seizure, tumor, anything. It seems likely it was a blood sugar swing, a kind of traveling hypoglycemia.

The lesson was clear; one should always bring Chinese carry-out, specifically spare ribs, when first visiting Israel. Who knew?

1991 - HOW IT HAPPENED - MY FIRST VISIT TO POLAND AND LEARNING SMUGGLING

Poland. Who went there? Why even think about it? I mean, it was 1991; the darkness of Soviet occupation was still everywhere. There was virtually no economy, and so little promise, even, at that time. With my few trips to this date I wasn't exactly well traveled, so why pick Poland? I actually had a damn fine reason, quite apart from the roots business I mentioned at the start of my travels. And this visit became the mental jumping off point for all the many travels that followed, and for the wondrous experience with Gosia.

My mother, born in 1897 and now 94, had lived alone in her home in New York City since my father died. I had been back and forth to New York from my home in Virginia just about every three weeks since the mid-eighties, kind of wearing on me, my job and my car. All during the late eighties she and I wrestled with her care and the usual business of what to do - where she should be? It was all too apparent that the time would come, if she lived, that a move to our home in McLean, outside Washington, would happen.

But she wanted to stay put as long as possible. And she was quite competent, even with physical frailty. So we went through perhaps 15 to 20 caregivers there in her neighborhood; she tolerant, me going nuts trying to do this 250 mile away stuff and having no feel whatsoever for what was right and good for her.

An ad showed up in the local, very local, neighborhood paper, The Wave, a long time Rockaway Beach clotch of local beach-type news. A woman, a Polish woman as it turned out, wanted caregiving work.

And so it was Teresa Piechocka, in 1985 I recall, came into our lives. I think it makes sense, as Polish names come up, to offer a quick note on pronouncing the key names. While the language is tough to learn, pronunciation and sounding of words is a walk in the park. This surprises everyone. Teresa is with soft e's…eh. Piechocka is quite simply Peehohtska.

It was Teresa's ad. She lived with her son in his Rockaway Beach home, was in her fifties and like so many Poles in the U.S. would do almost anything to make some money, dollars to keep or send home in someone's sock. Again, like many, Teresa was an educated woman; caring for the elderly was just something she did of necessity. In Poland this was a fact of life. So many homes were crowded and multi-generational. Seven or eight family members in three rooms was almost commonplace. No big deal if you've always lived it.

Teresa became the key to prolonging my mother's life comfortably. For us she found Halina Zukowska, who was with us for years, Emilia, Janina, Maria, Basia, Jadza, another Halina and the incredible Danuta Jurchak, Dana, who came to Virginia with us when we finally moved my mother. I don't recall all their vocations, but there were two doctors, one veterinarian and Dana was a college trained chemist. All were skilled caregivers; all had been there before at home. It was just the most natural thing. And it was also a job. Mixed in with this crowd was one Mary, a young Irishwoman from this great New York neighborhood.

It was 1990. The deal was working but still I was back and forth all the time. Teresa had signaled she would be going back home for a short visit, but not to worry her daughter-in-law was in town and would pinch hit. The system of rotating, incredibly wonderful caregivers would live on.

I should say that these women were for the most part...physical...and some were even...um...large. This pleased my mom; she feared falling and knew one or another strong Pole would be there to pick her up and deposit her in the nearest chair.

Well. Teresa is gone, off to Poland. Her replacement to work Teresa's own hours is due to come by just to meet us. The daughter-in-law.

I'm sitting on the front porch, deep in smug, reading my *NY Times*, and I happen to look up and see a bike with a kid approaching. So what. Well, the bike stops in front of my home and what looks like a quite pretty but quite skinny 14 year old girl pops off.

Meet the daughter-in-law, Danuta Piechocka, all 5 foot and some 105 pounds of her. Red flag. She bounces up the stairs, says hi, seats herself, and I'm floored. What to do? My mother would think this a bad joke. Never mind that this

young woman - she was 30 - had two daughters of her own.
Never mind that she was a prodigious musician, as we later
discovered…she was tiny!

She could never drag an old woman needing help
around the house. Even bathing my mother was dangerous,
what with the old fashioned step over bath tub. No way.
And why, I again asked myself, did I get to make these great
decisions? No biggee, one just did as one felt best with no
regrets later. All families deal with it, nothing at all special.

So Danuta - many called her Danka - came into
our lives…(Danka is sounded "Donka" with the o as in say
ah.) She reminded me right off that I had met her husband,
Marek, a year or two earlier. Teresa had not reminded me…
Marek Piechocki, Teresa's son.

Then came a big oops - gap in caregivers.

Danuta left us; was gone about a month later. She
says she left of her own volition. My mom never accepted
this caregiving peanut, and Danka spent all her free time on
the Steinway playing and singing. She did both, beautifully.
But…I mean…this was a job! Cook! Clean! Wash! Sit and
talk to her old woman! A job! This was the first time my
mother really rebelled.

So, in Teresa's absence her daughter-in-law left us.
Quit. Whatever. Gone. She had sensed the uneasiness with
my mother. It had to end.

Early the next year I moved my mother to our
Virginia home. Teresa came with us to aid in the transition, to
keep some continuity for my mom. Teresa, I might just add,
was not exactly healthy herself, suffering from rheumatoid

arthritis for years. Suffering pretty much silently, when around me at least.

Teresa reminded me that I not only had partial Polish roots but that I now had a good reason to visit Poland. I had learned some Polish of necessity, and now had many Polish friends and acquaintances. Danuta and Marek invited me and off I went. That's how it happened.

Thus it was that in June of 1991 I flew to Berlin's Tegel airport, where Marek and his brother-in-law, Krzysztof, met me. "Krzysztof" can be a tough one...say it Shyshtof and be done with it. The "y" as in "in".

Poland, only a year or so removed from Soviet occupation.

They were double parked and hustled me outside in a big hurry. Ok so far, I had my tour guides, my...uh...lifeline.

Their car, an elderly, creepy communist-built something, was down on its shocks if indeed it had any. I picked up on the reason as they jammed me into the back seat. It seems they had raided every store and shop in Berlin and I was to keep watch on hundreds of dollars of marginally legal goods of all descriptions, all for re-sale in Poland. It was in fact a way of life at that time, just a few years after the Berlin wall came down. People, those who could, did this.

Ok, so I'm a bit nervous. But I was tired from the flight. I tried to just put it out of mind. I was but an innocent passenger.

The Polish border is really but about an hour's drive from Berlin if one knew the way. Problem was getting through. We were maybe 10 miles away when we began to see trucks, semi's and everything imaginable, stopped on the right side. It was June and the drivers were just standing about, half dressed, obviously killing time. This was 1991, crossing the border was still not easy, and these guys were in for a wait that could last for two or three days…yep, two or three days. This route - Berlin, Poznan, Warsaw and on through Belarus to Moscow or wherever - was the main east, west highway in northern Europe. It carried virtually all the cargo across that part of Europe. It was jammed.

For passenger vehicles it wasn't quite so bad. We slipped past the trucks and really didn't have to slow until we were maybe a kilometer from the German border police. I dozed, I had to.

Ok, we were through the German side. No problems at all.

But I did have some doubts about the Polish side. We were carrying I have no idea how much value in goods that ought to be declared at any border. And I was sitting right in the middle of it all - just an innocent babe of course. A bit on edge.

Krzysztof it seems had been through this more than once. In fact, he had been through lots more than this; he had even been imprisoned, I found out later, for defying the police during Communist times on some currency suspicion and had spent a year in prison. A big believer in authority he was not. He loathed it, in fact. Hat off to you, K.

So what else could we do but what we did?. He pulled out around the backed up dozen or so vehicles awaiting clearance, and took off into Poland. I about died. This so naive American now an accomplice to smuggling. Oh well.

POZNAN, POLAND - JUNE 1991 AND FREE AFTER ALMOST 20 YEARS OF OCCUPATION

To set context for those who don't know, Poland had known but 21 years of freedom since the time of our own revolution - since the 1770s - and almost up until the Berlin wall came down. Poland was parceled out in the late 18th century, and re-divided twice more, between Prussia/Germany, Russia and Austria. It simply ceased to exist as a nation. Only during the years 1918 to 1939 did it know freedom. Then it was destroyed. And then occupied again. Free 21 years since about 1776. Think about this. And think about it again.

Not a thing happened. No one followed. Nothing. We sped off east.

There were three, mmm four, notable things about the remaining three or so hours needed to reach Poznan.

First, the roads themselves. They were two lane, each with a narrow, horse cart width, shoulder. That seemed to make some sense. But each lane had deep ruts, in that our Communist friends had neglected to put down a decent base and this was, as I said, the major east-west artery. Repeatedly we had one set of tires or the other caught in these deep truck

ruts, and had to throw the steering wheel over just to get out.
Fun. A new thrill.

Another new thrill. More than once, going over a
slight rise or around a bend, three cars would be coming at
us - both lanes and the opposite shoulder. This left for us only
the narrow horse cart sized shoulder on our side. Most often
after dark you couldn't even see if our shoulder might have
a cart on it. This was not your average thrill; this scared the
bejesus out of this American smuggler. In fact, it's scary just
to recall it. The two guys up front didn't seem to notice.

Something also quite new to me were the prostitutes
working the side of the road, literally every few kilometers.
They were, I was told, almost all from southeast Europe,
Bulgaria or Romania. Behind them in the woods you could
see one or two cars, the work place and often the carefully
watching…supervisor. Seems this was big money, hundreds
of truck drivers. A new culture for me and I have no idea
how good people traveled with young kids. I guess it was
openly talked about.

Oh yes…the best. The guys stopped twice at my
asking, for the most incredible roadside grilled kielbasa…
For me this alone made the drive worthwhile.

We made it to Poznan; ruts, head-on almosts and all.
With our two hundred pounds or so of smuggled goods we
were in and ready to sell.

Marek and Danuta Piechoccy lived on an attractive,
beautifully treed street toward the western side of the city.
I had no idea what to expect as their home, but it was just
as warm and attractive as could be. They had one of two of

what we would call townhouses, attached, with a staircase dividing the two dwellings. Each had three floors, each floor of maybe 600 square feet having been a full family apartment in earlier years. Marek, a graphics artist by trade but with a flair for home design, had built and installed an interior circular staircase to enable up and down without using the common inside staircase. It was very graceful and eye catching. Rooms were all good town house sized, but for the kitchen being a bit cramped. A very beautiful back garden by the way, with several different fruit and nut trees and vines. The water was not then potable, full of heavy metals from many Communist era factories.

This so warm and attractive home had been home, also, for officers of the occupying German army during the war. I slept in the living room, a room back then slept in by soldiers of a nation not known for its humanity. This weighed far more heavily on me than it did my hosts, not surprisingly. They knew this story quite well.

Catching the eye inside too were Marek's 2000 bottle caps, in multiple panels on the dining room wall. His wife enjoyed these so much, in her dining room. Marek to this day still collects, up over 5000 I hear. (Now, in 2008, he has 6000 different bottle caps!)

A bit more interesting to me were the two daughters, Krysia the older by 17 months, and Gosia. Ten and nine in 1991. They were even then so pretty; tall and skinny, one light, the other darker, and I quickly noticed quite full of opinions. More about these girls, much more, later. Living with them was the wonderful and fiery Mietek, Danuta's dad, a guy I came to understand a little over the years. He came to call me the best Jew since Moses, and he for me was second only to the Polish Pope - our little nonsense joke but important to me.

I had wondered about Poznan as we drove in. It seemed to have wide and comfortable streets, not at all what I thought to expect in Poland. But Poznan had been the German Posen up until just after the first World War ended in the west, when the Poles rose up and claimed it. Like so many cities in western Poland it had the spacious and well laid out feeling of German cities. It was, however, dirty; not so much the streets but the buildings. This was the inevitable result of years of burning the very worst coal, with its airborne pollution. Even in June one could smell it. Buildings everywhere were gray and dark. The Soviet legacy was one of horrible air and water pollution.

The city itself was dark at night. It was too soon after the suffocating Soviet presence for much night time activity. There was hardly any advertising, and very few restaurants were to be seen even during the day.

There was, though, a charming old market in the old city - the Stary Rynek in the Stary Miasto. An open space with the city hall in the center, and shops surrounding. It had of course been rebuilt, although Poznan did not suffer the devastation of, for example, Warsaw.

Marek was trying his serious first post-communist job, as a graphics artist for an office supply house. Danuta taught music. I had no idea she taught so much music; piano, violin, guitar, voice, choir. Their girls attended the usual elementary school; and after that studied music…piano, voice and maybe more…I don't recall.

This was a quite welcoming and hard working, by any standard I knew, family. And I found out pretty early on they were also serious animal lovers, Krysia more so than anyone I knew but perhaps for myself. Their dog, then, was Bingo, a feisty, lovable Kerry Blue terrier.

Ok, this Polish town was easy to understand and the family was musical, educated and just great.

What impressions from this first visit? Well, certainly the dearth of store front lights, no food or clothing stores anything like western super stores, hardly any restaurants to be seen, and no cars newer, it seemed, than 1970 or so. And the lingering and ever present pollution, both air and water. The public transport was interesting; trams and trolleys dating back to the mid century.

But I had in fact chosen to come in June for a reason. This was the month for the annual Poznan International Trade Fair, described by Teresa as very well known and very well attended. An international trade fair in Poland? Of all places - the very much still non-market Poland?

Amazingly, it was indeed impressive, with as much space as anything like it in a New York or Washington convention center. All manner of consumer and industrial goods were offered, in beautiful floor and booth displays. This was not of communist roots…how in the world could it be, so soon? I never really could figure this, even with my own training in business and economics. I think now I was seeing an explosion of pent up, suppressed creation; these business folks had been storing ideas for years.

This fair contrasted so dramatically with everything else. Something was about to happen in this nation that had suffered so much.

So, this first visit to Poland had been very special. I had been an accessory to smuggling, enjoyed rut-ridden roads with innumerable roadside working women, met a family as western as any in the States, seen close up an economy just emerging from a dark age, met some who would play a big time role in my future, sampled wonderful food prepared in a still very basic kitchen, seen contrasts close up…and most important had my appetite further whetted.

A good idea, this short trip.

ITALY 1992 - A GIRL OR A DOG?

Go see for yourself. I can say little of Italy and
everyone else can say so much. Or read any of the thousands
of books that sell like mad. This visit was so short that even
impressions were hard to come by. I was visiting on business
the town of Lerici, on the coast a bit south of Genoa. Very
close to the storied Tuscan countryside.

Other than the much anticipated great food,
incredible hillsides of flowers and homes, beautifully dressed
everyone, views of the warm sea and always in the eastern
sky, mountains, even the Carrara mountainside marble, the
long winding line of traffic behind one heavy woman on a
bike, all the usual - only one incident recalls to mind.

I was walking the shoreline, a paved overview looking
down on massive boulders where people sunned. It was
truly storybook pretty - the sea, the rocks, the town and the
mountains to the east. But, as I've mentioned more than once,
I love dogs. And there he was, down some twenty feet on one
huge boulder, a marvelous looking big Lab type just lying
there and looking proud of his Italian self. I stared. I watched
him. I stared some more.

After maybe ten minutes of much admiring and
watching, his owner sat up and looked at me. And looked at
me. My business friend, walking with me and who knew Italy
better than I did, suggested we kind of slip away. I asked
why. He said that guy doesn't much like you staring at his
girl friend. He may be about to take big time offense.

I hadn't noticed her at all, fully reclined, and fully
topless. Supine she looked like a guy. Smart me. We bugged out.

Sorry…that's it for Italy.

Poznan to Warsaw 1992 -
The Importance of a Smooth Bottom

At sixes and sevens job-wise myself and coming to love the mystery and feel of central Europe, I thought I'd look to promote something that might grow as Poland's economy turned west. The import export business was no mystery to me, at least in theory. I'd taught it and a few years before was a partner in a Sears management consulting subsidiary, the very classy and highly thought of Harbridge House, where we offered a range of services to U.S. and overseas firms. One of the major Japanese trading houses had been a personal client of mine. Maybe, I thought, I could catch a budding Polish idea, help them and position myself to be a part of a growing operation. Even get some of my travel funded.

Marek Piechocki, himself looking hard during these formative years of the Polish market economy, of his economy, arranged maybe 15 meetings for us both. One was with a set of business and university people at which I met another major influence on my future ties to Poland - Walery Lach, a professor of economics and marketing at Poznan University. (Walery is sounded as with a V - Valery.)

Think about this, too, for a moment, someone teaching marketing. What in hell was marketing in Communist Poland? There was no such thing. Yet for the sake of students and to further the appeal of the wonders of centralized brain management, something had to be taught.

This could easily have been the world's briefest text book, yet assuredly it was not. It probably ran 1000 pages, all drivel. Still, with his boss, a Professor Mruk, it was taught.

Walery was then in a period of very difficult transition to the teaching of market economics, with virtually no free market textbook in Polish available to him and his colleagues. Nice isn't it, being deprived of mind for some 45 years? To his uncommon even courageous credit, he found an American marketing text and used it.

On my own I had arranged before I arrived a visit to a new office products firm, in Warsaw. Warsaw in 1991. Rebuilt by design with Soviet money and Communist good will. The very same Warsaw that had, as much as any city, known the horrors of WW II. Some 90% destroyed, block by block, by the Germans and then the Soviets. The two major uprisings, in the Jewish ghetto in 1943 and then the city as whole in 1944 while the Soviet army happily watched Poles and Germans killing one another added a final touch to the overall destruction.

But to show its love for Poland the Soviet Union designed and funded the construction of the huge cultural center in the midst of downtown Warsaw. A sun blocking monster of a multi-tiered building, revered by the Poles as the only place from which to see the building itself.

From anywhere else, from any other tall building, it was visible. From inside it itself you could not see it. This was best. A standing joke in Warsaw. It remains of course, still - not quite as despised as in 1991 with Russians now pretty much long gone.

I might just add an aside. I now know many Poles and almost to a man and woman they despise the mindlessness of the Soviets and Communism more than they hated the memory of Nazi horrors. One was over quickly, but the other was insidious and lingered. Maybe this is just the passage of time, but not from what I know and have read. Of course Stalin allegedly said that Communism fitted Poland as a saddle might a cow. Perhaps it was a camel, I've heard it both ways.

Marek and I sought out and found that office products firm, located on Mila Street (the street made famous in Leon Uris' "Mila 18", his story of the ghetto uprising against the Nazi occupiers in 1943). It lay in the heart of the totally destroyed and rebuilt former ghetto. I can't really describe the feeling I had - it was somewhere between can this be and what I knew to be. And I was standing there.

The owners of this firm were maybe 25 years of age each. Two young men, beautifully dressed and driving I soon saw two unlikely cars for 1992 Poland - a bright red Corvette and a top line BMW. Hm?? Big money so soon?? How?

The store was as well equipped as any office supply house then in the States would be. Upscale copiers, fax machines, furniture, computers of that time…the whole works. A few million dollars in inventory for certain. And this was Poland just a short while removed from Communist blessings.

There was absolutely no doubt that these two young business men had family Communist ties. The cars alone proved that. Seems like Communism had its good side, for the chosen few. We did almost do a deal, on environmental products, but it fell afoul politics wherein I was way out of my league. Potentially dangerous politics in fact.

But Marek, recall, had a family back in Poznan. His wife and two pre-teen daughters. Care to guess what he bought for them? Poles always do gifts. I mean always. Marek did the best gift imaginable - 3 cases of toilet paper. I kidded him big time about this and then realized what a fool I was. The TP I then remembered they had back home was brown, rough, awful stuff, maybe a notch up from exfoliated river birch bark. He did a very great thing for his three women. Thus the importance of being un-scratchy, of a smooth bottom.

It seemed that the joys and contrasts of Communism reached deep and wide, touching randomly. No...not randomly at all.

I did also see for the first time the various monuments to the war spread throughout that forever abused, storied city. The two that tore me up were the one memorializing the 1944 uprising, a young boy, maybe ten, carrying a rifle and wearing a much oversized helmet; and the Umschlagplatz, the loading point for Jews being sent to Treblinka.

Don't bother with the Holocaust Museum unless you go to Warsaw first. Then as I did, and will describe, see a few other concentration and death camps. Then maybe the museum if you need more. You shouldn't.

The South of Poland - 1993

Yes, just a year later. No excuse to go this time. I was simply fed up looking for a good job; I'd had several bad ones quite recently and was living major disenchantment trying to find something with both challenge and opportunity. I was almost 60 and not the hottest young prospect around. Jobs were to be had but I had no wish to associate with idiots - some dishonest and caught and others just sleazy - like those I'd been around for a few years. Earlier I'd had a strong measure of very good jobs, both in and out of government. I'd been privileged to work with some well known people of high principle.

Maybe I was enjoying my own early old age crisis. Had I stayed long enough with any one of the good jobs, some reminded me, I'd had have it made by now. But for me no end was an end; always a means, not a good thing. Always a professional dilettante, a tough way to earn a reputation or even a living for sure.

So I just up and decided to ask if I might visit my Poznan friends. The answer was a little slow in coming back, by fax in those prehistoric days, in that it was Easter, a time of both reverence and I quickly found out travel. Marek met me in Berlin again and announced that whether I liked it or not we were bugging out to the south, the Silesian mountains right at the Czech border, to go skiing.

Just what I did not want. I only wanted to sit and think about my need for a job. With a family history of skiing in some of the best locations the states had to offer, east and west, the south of Poland didn't really light my fire. No Stowe or Aspen there. Also this region of Poland I knew had even more limited telephone service than did the bigger cities and I had to stay in touch. In fact, you needed to wake an operator to make any call at all.

And so I found myself in a very rustic, I do mean rustic, very cold part of southern Poland. Food I didn't understand too well, a bare bones room by my rich American ski lodge standards, hardly anyone to talk to when the family skied, still no job and no way to get in touch with things back in the States. This was another of those what the hell am I doing here deals, much like the bus to East Berlin.

We went to church late one night, about 11. Marek is very religious and it was Easter week. We were it, the only ones there. It was primitive really, maybe 300 years old. There was no heat; maybe 25 or 30 degrees Fahrenheit. I recall looking at his wife and the girls repeatedly…thinking don't they realize this is overdoing it? No sign from them. In Poland, a deeply religious nation, and for good reason, this was routine stuff. I watched while Marek did what he did hoping silently this would end fast. I'd attended church with him several times before, but this one was painful. Finally we left, back to our heated lodgings, walking of course on dark mountain roads.

For me the puzzle of religion had added a quick extra dimension. I of course know many Catholics. Some I count as very good friends over the years. But here we mixed this question of organized, wealthy religion, about which I've spoken, with very personal devotion. It was no problem at all for Marek. He saw no disconnect at all between the overwhelming wealth of the Church and his feelings. He accepted his station as it was, fully knowing his Church had amassed billions of dollars. Did he accept? Or was he fearful? Was it all rote and passed down from religious parents? I saw an easy ability to not think too much about all this. He would not talk of it.

Now, as I write, I think his wife and grown daughters still accept his views as they did then. We all accept family. But I don't think they are as tolerant of no discussion. My family would certainly come down on me hard if I could not explain my feelings of something so meaningful, impacting so on our personal lives and this world of religious conflict. Deeply held convictions more than ever are the root cause of conflict. Like it or not.

But I had something else to mull over. I was a target! As we walked up and down the hillsides, with quite rudimentary roads, one old car repeatedly made a half-hearted run at me. I'd be tossing a ball with Krysia, or watching Gosia's flying feet on the rocks, and here came this car, having run to the top, aiming kind of poorly with happy purpose at me. Marek finally stopped this guy and asked him what the hell was going on.

Vodka was one thing going on. Rural and usually poor Poles started drinking early. What he had in his besotted mind was just clipping me gently. He thought I was German, he told Marek, no idea I was American. Marek got him to bag it.

So I survived. And later I even managed an accident with the family car one day while they were skiing. I slid off a road on ice. Fun trying to find a Polish tow vehicle in a most remote mountain setting.

Finally I'd had enough. I asked my hosts could I
bug out. Prague was quite close and an easy air connection
was possible. They said no so back to Poznan some 7 hours
we trekked, then another day, and then another 5 hours to
Berlin. Only time lost. I guess they liked me. In truth each
moment I spent in Poland added a little more feel for this
nation and its people who have borne so much.

No job, no job contacts, much literally cold-blooded
religion, walking prey for an angry drunk driver, a car
accident with AAA 4000 miles away...an awful waste of time
some might say. Not hardly. Smart? No, just an escape, not
too expensive. More for my growing store of the lands of my
parents' forebears.

Warsaw 1996 - Monuments to Heroism

Warsaw had changed. All of urban Poland was
changing. Lights were coming on. No longer were there
so few retail shops. Even in the countryside as I found in
exploring, business activity was much more in evidence.
Advertising almost nonexistent in 1991 was everywhere.
Even cars were newer and certainly more abundant. Warsaw
was not yet the traffic brother of New York or DC, which it
did indeed become by time of my early 2000 visits, but you
could feel it coming - an eastern European need to catch up
fast - to attempt any and all of what the heavy Soviet fist had
denied since 1945.

This city has a pervasive music culture. It isn't only Chopin, there are of course many Polish composers. But still the feel for Chopin is all about. Music is to be found everywhere, as we found it to be a few years later in Prague. Every small hall, every church almost, will offer classical concerts covering all the masters. For me it had the feel again of returning, of seeing almost the birth of much of 17th to 19th century classical music. Sorry - I know I tend to overplay my reaction to some of what I was experiencing but you either do or you don't. Stop reading any time you like, or you stay with it and perhaps share with me some of this emotion. Your decision.

Well, I did need a hotel. I was giving a talk on a major environmental issue, the question of coal combustion and its risks. That was me at that time, an assessor of environmental risks. It was new to me as a discipline, but the U.S. government didn't care. I was it. What the hell it was only coal, the biggest energy polluter going - who needed to know anything. Cheers for the U.S. Environmental Protection Agency.

Where was this meeting? The Warsaw Marriott Yep, the Marriott now in Warsaw. This hotel was elegant in every way, as much so as any four or five star here. It was a shocker for this uninitiated traveler - Marriott of course was legendary amongst innovative hotel chains but how in the world had Poland come so far so fast?

It had. Stalin had been so right. That Communist saddle was indeed a bad idea from the start. Polish entrepreneurship was everywhere.

So I knuckled under. I took my residence there. But taxpayer you may be thankful - my room was paid for by industry. The U.S. EPA approved this conflict of interest, in writing. Whoops?

You wonder how I could take industry money? Let me say for the record that the U.S. EPA relied exclusively on industry for all of the technical data it used in assessing that *very same* industry. This was an old EPA practice and sheer nonsense. I did make the argument from time to time that any analysis performed with this information, which also was so thin as to not pass any Statistics 101 laugh test, was ethically and scientifically insupportable. But I stayed on. Fight from inside. And the mortgage payment.

Polish trains. I'd read of them only heading east. To various camps. But in truth they went everywhere and did their job well as is the case all through the Europe I know. But it's always fun buying a ticket from someone with whom you can't speak and then seeing all kinds of notes and scratching on this ticket to where you hope to go. I could have bought through the Marriott concierge for only a 60% add-on fee and had confidence. No way. So off to the Warsaw station, a few blocks away to buy a ticket west, back to the Poznan I'd come to know.

In a Polish city the main train station is called the Glowny, with the city name preceding. This gets important unless you don't care if you get off in some far off suburb and get to do the whole bit again, in Polish or Croatian or whatever. Big sign out front...Warsaw Centralna, the Warsaw Glowny but by a different name.

Even in Warsaw the ticket seller did not speak English. But I did the ticket and then spend an hour or so reading all arrival and departure boards clueing in on Polish for track, time and whatever. Made a few visits to various tracks and it all checked out. Trains came and went as I'd figured.

On arriving, after passing the first Poznan station hoping I'd got the Glowny bit right, the station is jammed. Where the hell is Walery Lach, to pick me up? Hitting me hard more in surprise than anything was the sight of an orthodox Jew, maybe a rabbi, amongst all these very, I do mean very, non-Jewish Poles. I thought…this guy has courage…could I do that?

Maybe for him it was nothing. I mean - there were then perhaps depending on how you count 5000 Jews remaining of 3 million. A little over one for every thousand before. Why should he stand out? He was certain of his popularity, his high standing.

One more train story. I had to get back to Berlin a few days later for my flight, leaving about noon. This meant a very early train, like 3 am. No problem, there I was on board. Not my seat, not the right car, but a seat. The 63 year old American enjoying the company at 3 am of a ton of much younger, big and rough looking Poles…workers heading off to so attractive Germany to earn a pay check. A bit uncomfortable for me but this is how one does it…one just does it.

As we approach the German border the train slows, stops, and Polish border police come aboard. Each is dressed almost as for a costume party; tattered, unpressed even dirty uniforms, slovenly shoes, unshaven. Each carries a pencil and some note paper. Well…a Polish job I guess.

We cross the border and stop again. Here come the German passport control guards. Their uniforms were two tone and pressed, boots shined, eyes clear, freshly shaven of course. Each carried a mid nineties notebook computer.

So you see…a so slight societal difference. One subsisting, one prospering. Neighbors. I'm both, Polish and German. It seems God had a purpose here at the border, to confuse me. He wanted all us travelers to witness for ourselves how all men are created equal. What am I missing about all this?

BERLIN AND POZNAN - 1998; THE THRILL OF NO LANES FOR YOU

Forget driving Miss Daisy, travels with Charley, Kerouac. This time I'd planned on doing a bunch of driving myself. You get me. Marginally literate but me.

Again, if Mary and I had been smart enough to wander Europe as newlyweds on the U.S. Army's nickel I'm pretty sure much of this old age stuff might have been avoided. Of course, it might have worked the other way; I might have the bug even worse.

Tegel Airport in Berlin as usual and I rented a car, a really neat Opel Vectra. This was a car that would sell now big time here with gas prices finally moving. This was no cheap Opel from the 60's; it was a sharp middle of the line smallish vehicle, a solid GM product in Europe. Sweet metallic silver, stick of course. It moved too.

I had only one problem with this car. Mr. Big making his speedy way through northern Europe forgot how the gear shift worked. So...there I was a little lost in eastern Germany on a roundabout, a traffic circle, headed in the wrong direction and unable to back up...I had to...no other way.

The silly gear shift had a reverse arrow - I'm glad to say this did catch my clever eye - but the stick wouldn't go there. Stupid German car. What do they do, never back up? Of course, there is no such car as a stupid German car.

Well, I imagine you've figured this one out. You simply slipped your fingers around the gear stick at the cross bar and lifted. It worked so smoothly once the brain clicked in.

I might admit I had this same brain lock problem about six years later, with a Renault, trying desperately to back into a parking place in Paris so the aging bladder might empty itself real fast. This problem, that of finding a bathroom on instant notice, became both a real concern and more than once an embarrassment. What the hell, this wasn't going to stop me, one could always change.

I got backing up help from a Frenchman who, speaking English well, had a great little story himself to tell of the American who could not only not shift for himself but who ran quite strangely into that Chinese restaurant holding a dollar in his hands - a toilety bribe which happily worked with about one second to spare.

Back to my drive to Poznan.

This was my first time driving these Polish roads at speed. I'd prepared myself mentally. Must watch not only the oncoming lanes, all 15 of them, but also the rear view mirror for the Indy guys bearing down on me. In Europe you use that mirror and use it continuously or you pack it in. Not like here at all. It's driving, not like on our interstates in any sense.

I came to enjoy it actually. Germany was the usual, you stay in your chosen lane or changed and got back. Poland uh uh, no chosen lane, all lanes are fair game. I was still a softball shortstop and eye-hand-eye coordinated and made it easily and ho hum just another drive to Poznan in about 4 hours even with the border. But exciting, believe me.

Now to find the house. I'd thought I knew enough of the city and I got real lucky. Entering Poznan from the west things change as pretty much here in the States. Rural roads to more signs and more everything. And the Polish road signs were everywhere and quite easy to read, in kilometers of course. I exited the incoming highway on a guess and found myself right on Dombrowskiego Steet… ulica Dombrowskiego, the main boulevard leading to ul. Niemcziewica where I needed to be.

This is very good when it happens, a lucky turnoff in a foreign language city. So, unerring and modestly suave, I chugged in at 4:30 and dinner was waiting.

I'll get back to the driving in a moment. But I'd like to again mention Krysia and Gosia in passing here. They were 17 and 16 about and now quite grown up teenagers. Poised,

educated, graceful and as opinionated as ever. Especially
Krysia on the opinionated. Gosia held many, boys included,
at arms length. The thought of inviting one or both to study
in the States had long before crossed my mind, although I'd
had no experience at arranging any of that...school, host
family, health insurance, any of it.

We were all waiting at dinner, but for Gosia upstairs
still. She came bouncing down, carrying an architecture text
book and a drawing pad. We all did the usual conversation
at dinner, best we could in English, with Gosia reading her
homework, sketching as she read and chatted while eating
her dinner. Then without a word, we're still eating, she stood
up and zipped into the music room, the living room, closed
the door and exploded on the piano into super fast Bach and
I don't recall what else. Her sister looked bored, her Dad
the same, and her Mom the so talented musician herself just
smiled a little and said Gosia has great technique.

I'd witnessed something special. A young person of
strength of character, wonderful mind and incredible focus,
just doing what came so naturally. I thought I knew Krysia
pretty well, but this was my first real insight into Gosia.
When I say well I mean just from fun visits, talking dogs a
bit, playing ball and thinking often of what I might offer to
these girls. My feeling right then was that I had to ask if I
might bring one of them to the States for a semester or two,
to find a way to make this happen if they wished it so. Krysia
or Gosia, no matter to me. I felt sure that either, both, would
do quite well.

I am seriously saddened about all this only in that
I was not able to bring Krysia as well. She demurred and
Gosia said yes. I mean what I say, Krysia, should you ever
read this. I know you did Finland and other exciting things,

as you wished, and were best friend to Deni your incredible
Great Dane. But still I wish you'd been able to come with
your sister or alone. Next life. If you might allow me.

But back to that trip as I'd planned it. I was headed
west, much west, to Paris. I was what the hell bound to do
what I should have done years ago...drive Europe!

I mentioned Paris to the family. They had no idea of
my plans except that I was to travel somewhere. No one had
anything to say and even Danuta, the only real talker in this
bunch, was quiet.

She was thinking. I mean, was she ever thinking.
Next day she asked me if I might drive her, share driving
with her, to Germany right on my way if her husband ok'd it.
Just like that. She'd take off. Her best childhood friend lived
somewhere near Bonn, impossibly far away in expense terms.
She wanted to go. She asked Marek, he ok'd it, we were off a
couple of days later.

POZNAN TO BONN TO PARIS - 1998 AND DRIVING WITH ME NOT MISS DAISY

First off I couldn't share driving. She wasn't on the German rental and I didn't want to take a chance. I debated it all the way but decided against it.

But we stayed with the plan, to make it early on back to Berlin and with the autobahn getting south and west to Bonn to her friend by maybe dinner. We hit the road six am or so. For me this was the second leg of this adventure I'd postponed so long, for her just a way to get there. Her family had driven Europe for years even during the dismal days of Communism. I do know this was the best car she'd ever seen close up. In fact Marek borrowed it, loved it, during the time in Poznan.

Well we got close. It was maybe 5 pm and I couldn't find the town. I had vaguely located it in my mind trusting to find German signs but the town - Hangelar - never showed. No one knew the street name - Kapitalstrasse I think now - maybe longer. German streets can have long names.

Now - the first of so many wonderful, so warm and so surprising to some - incidents in this Germany friends tell me they just avoid.

We wandered into a neighborhood of very attractive, newer, modest seeming homes. It might have been Westchester, a bit down scale. A gentleman, older, near his front lawn. I stopped, waved and went over to him. I saw an almost useless withered right arm. I started to ask and he interrupted.

Why do you speak English? I was a bit pissed right off, and tired. I said well you know Americans have been here now for some time, fifty years, you speak English far better than we do German. He glared, clearly just generally tight.

Then, ever helpful and never bashful, Danuta came up and started in. This really got to him.

Where are you from, you're not American? Poland. Poznan. Poznan? Ha. You mean Posen. No, Poznan. It was Posen, he insisted.

It was becoming clearer. This guy, in his seventies I would judge, was a veteran of the war, had lost much of his arm on the horrific Russian front and now lived in a community of homes provided to war veterans. He meant no insult, he was just an old German soldier not exactly happy with being partially disabled for years, and jumped on by an American and a Pole. His best friends years before.

Well, guess what? His wife much younger came out, found us straightforward directions and he, not her, then invited us to come see his home. Inside this home, as pretty as might be, she then asked us to join them in their garden for coffee and dessert.

We did. We spent about an hour with this older German couple in a very beautiful setting. I can still see it and feel it. I really hope you can.

Peoples can't get along? Really? German hospitality, coffee, desserts?

One more story to tell of German warmth this trip.
A story of a strange banker and his staff. I'll make it just a
little shorter.

I'd gone into a bank in this town to change some
money. They knew of course I was no long term customer.
No one else was there, but for the manager and his staff.
I just started making small talk, I do this to learn when
traveling, rarely here at home. I talked with the three or four
tellers and after a few minutes the manager wandered out.
More back and forth talk about nothing. Ok…he'd had it.
He invited me into his office and asked me to please accept a
bottle of nice wine he just happened to have. More talk and
my thanks for just the great overall reception. A sales pitch?
This guy never saw me again.

Next day Danuta, her girlhood buddy Lydia (Lidka I
think) and I set off for Paris. They insisted, I caved. Andy's
Angels. Charley's Angels had been a hot TV program. Three
woman and a cop. I soon had my third, Isabelle again. Seven
more hours of my catchup driving.

Isabelle lived east of Paris, less than an hour, in a
town near EuroDisney. A village, homes crowded together,
chickens on the narrow streets, the not at all uncommon
French village. Her directions had been awful; the exit she
gave me was fine heading from Paris but did not exist coming
in from the east, from Germany. Sooo…a few u turns later
we found it. Thanks Isa. You've done this since again, after
you moved to your own house. I know you, I should have
figured this.

You blew it off. So? You want to see France, non?

That same night we all four plus Yves, Isabelle's house-sharing friend, set off for Paris. I wanted sleep, they all said I must be kidding. Paris it must be. Yves' English was the worst, unununderstandable. So of course he sat up front next to me. Ok getting to Paris, ok signs this time. In Paris and about midnight and when leaving this guy had me going nuts. One huge Swiss diplomatic plate car nearly broadsided my little Vectra.

Home. I slept. Be really careful with the French and cars.

We did the return to Bonn a few days later and I caught a plane from Frankfurt instead of driving all the way back to Berlin. I much appreciated Lufthansa changing my ticket at no cost. In fact the best friend I made on this trip was Lufthansa! Germany to Poland to Germany to France and back to Germany got it out of my system but good. More damn driving I did not need!

But what a blast. I can't believe I did all this, but I was much younger then, about 65.

PRAGUE 1998 - NUMBER ONE
FOR GOOD REASON

Prague for many years, even before the downfall of Soviet Russia, had gotten a ton of favorable press. It was a city of destination for many young Americans, almost in the way Paris was in the 1920s but without quite the gathering of the literati. Many of these kids stayed on. It became very easy to understand why they stayed. No question in my mind, this is the one city of all those I've seen that for any American traveler, anyone somewhat new to Europe, is a must visit.

Of course I know! I'm not the first to say this. Ease up.

It's truly glorious, the town and the beautiful river and many bridges, and relatively inexpensive - costs maybe one half here in the states. Truly an inexpensive Paris in many ways.

Incredible architecture; cafés, shops and restaurants everywhere; eye-catching, stretching water views, historical sites to blow your mind, music offered everywhere for about ten bucks per concert in close up venues, and now modern in spite of timeless beauty. It also stands at a European crossroads; maybe not a Vienna or Budapest in this sense but still a bridge to the troubling Slavic east and south.

It has a fully understandable and modern metro system. The signs were the best imaginable, very easy to follow without knowing a word of Czech. In the center of each car at the top and placed crosswise so you could see it from everywhere was the schematic of the line you were on showing where you were and going. You could sneak in of course as you can in many cities in Europe but you don't want to. It does its job too well. (Even on busses and trams and some above ground trains in Europe you can often do this. Not nice. Don't.)

I was there for another conference on environmental issues tying to coal. With me were two of my closest colleagues: Paul Ziemkiewicz and Ishwar Murarka. Paul headed West Virginia University's water research lab and Sir Ishwar of the Many Diplomas was a preeminent voice in the study of the risks associated with coal burning. It was a wonderful pleasure for me to travel with these two...both great guys and each taking a turn at keeping me straight technically.

Paul was kind of climbed over by a couple of female pickpockets late one night. He claimed he fought but we think he actually knew them. As they peeled off and left we saw him wave goodbye and then jot something down on a scrap of paper. He returned to the exact site one night later.

Mary was with us of course; no Prague without her. She out of the blue said she'd never seen so many great looking young people. So young Americans stayed? Wonder why.

I've mentioned the music, the restaurants. Find the music, explore for restaurants - many are several flights below ground. Just go look. See the old Jewish quarter. A few shops and the cemetery remain. Stacked graves several down in that space got very scarce. I suppose this may be found in urban sites from the past elsewhere but it was new to me. This entire quarter was but a tiny part of old Prague; now you might miss it completely unless you watch carefully.

To the north of Prague toward Germany is the town of Terazin. Under German occupation it was Teresienstadt. Named for the empress Maria Teresa of course. It was during the war a holding place, in effect a concentration camp with entire in-town multistory buildings housing displaced families en route to hell. Many of the buildings held mementos of the stay of families and individuals. One that really took hold on Mary and me was a collection of children's sketches.

Just outside the town itself was a wire enclosed detention and torture camp, with outdoor sleeping and holding cells about the size of a large shipping trunk; maybe 4' x 4' x 6'. It was the usual red brick, with the usual Arbeit Macht Frei sign - the Nazi way of making people feel at home. Winters in Czechoslovakia got cold of course, and people died from mal everything plus exposure. The camp had administrative and interrogation offices, all still open then to see. This was my first such camp, either concentration or killing. In later travels, as I'll describe, I made it to both Chelmno and Auschwitz.

I suggest a visit to Prague for glorious beauty and so much fun, followed by a look at Terazin to judge if you need more. Terazin is only about an hour's tour bus ride.

My plan was to go from Prague up to Wroclaw in Poland and I'd priced a ticket here in the States before going. I was told $60 as I recall. Well. I bought the same ticket for $10 in Prague. I really did. I asked the local ticket office about a hundred times are you kidding? Yes…$10 it was.

The train ride was interesting and a bit different for me. The train itself was clean to start out, but after a dozen or so commuter stops…filthy. Sadly. The direction was east, to the town of Pardubice, and then a turn north to Poland. Ok. East and then a turn north. A simple left turn.

No. Stay parked in Pardubice for maybe a half hour and then start moving back - in the direction from which you just came. Whoops? My ticket had been examined and punched. The destination was Wroclaw clearly set out. Hang tough. With my skilled Czech I had little choice.

Well, as you've guessed all was well; it was simply a matter of getting back to a switch to a northbound track. This has happened to me a few times since in small European towns. Always fun. But never like that first time.

The shorter distance to Poland took over twice the time to Pardubice, in that the route meant climbing and then descending the mountains in Silesia. Moving? Crawling in many places. And the countryside after leaving the mountains was not exactly the best; the very poor coal districts of southern Poland.

Still in all a wonderful experience. But if you try something like this do bring food and try beforehand to empty bladders and such. Be forewarned

One other experience, back in Prague, weighed on Mary and me. We were walking everywhere and decided to check out the train station as I always did before a journey from a new city. Right outside the station, sitting in a circle off to the side was a group of perhaps 15-20 gypsies...eating. Both adults and children. We were quite familiar with street people, with homeless people, and feel the usual helplessness when confronted by such unfortunates here in the States.

But this was different. This communal group in different attire and without knife and fork seemed almost of another world. I apologize for saying this, I really do. But surrounding a fire, truly no eating implements that I could see, on an urban street? Tearing away at some meat? We were really taken aback. Of course we soon realized we'd just seen something not too unusual in east central Europe.

These were in truth people like us - like us but from a wholly different cultural niche.

Do not miss Prague. Go more than once for sure.

COLOGNE, BONN AND FULDA - 2000; DEEP UNDERGROUND TRAVELS

Oh well, more Germany. My roots thing was taking on the routine, exactly what I wanted. Come and go and learn.

Had I begun to see ghosts? I'm not sure but I certainly was becoming more and more at home. For an upper, upper middle aged American who was just out exploring each day was a joy of sight and sound. Yes…it's only Germany but it was my father's family's homeland.

This was another business trip, this time to check out a huge area of German coal mines, surface mines, west of Cologne and running about up to Aachen on the western border. I was told this was the largest such geological formation in the world but for one in South America somewhere. It lay at the heart of German industrial needs for coal.

The issue was how to reclaim the mine lands safely; something, oddly enough, I could never get my employer, the U.S. EPA, the slightest bit interested in even though we here in the U.S. have many thousands of such sites needing cleanup. My problems with EPA ran deep; I did not feel this Agency was politically strong enough to do what environmental trust mandated it do - indeed what Congress had mandated it do. The dangerously competent and devious Bush administration did not help.

Certainly coal was to be with us for awhile - no one doubted that. But there were ways to make the mining and combustion of coal safer. We in government were strangely powerless but industry having read all the signals had at least begun a series of programs that were helpful. Odd but true. My personal position was always in between. I was a not-to-be-trusted EPA risk assessor, to industry, and I constantly rattled my boss's cage while doing little to please environmentalists. Don't go work at EPA if you expect results. In addition to all I've said, lawyers know the game too well now to allow anything to happen. (As I write in 2008, I hope this may change.)

Let me add, as I comment on my work at EPA, that I never did find a risk at the legally *hazardous* level associated with the disposal of coal combustion by-products, the solid ash-like wastes. Of course these materials, like most bulk materials, can be toxic and ought not to be dumped just anywhere and especially near pristine water - but if properly managed seemed to be ok. In fact I came to be a strong believer in their use for coal mine reclamation as described just above. I never could accept the wastes being dumped into storage ponds.

Please excuse the above aside. Environmental work can be quite frustrating.

The Cologne cathedral? Immense and packed into an urban downtown. Worth seeing? Not for me. Try the many in the German and French countryside, like Reims, or even Notre Dame. Cologne is beautifully situated on the Rheine but so are dozens of beautiful cities and towns. It showed me little. Sorry. I'm sure there's more there than I could appreciate.

Bonn on the other hand I liked. This was my second visit and I enjoyed the smaller town feel, the history of cold war capital, the wonderful central market and the nearby Altstadt a kind of upscale but older apartment and café area. Reminded me a little of Georgetown in Washington, DC. Bonn also is on the Rheine of course and I did my first Rheine cruise on this visit.

Out of town just a short tram ride was the Konrad Adenauer home, then and now a national monument. Adenauer of course was post war Germany's first leader, and as important to the recovery of Germany's place among peaceful nations as any political personality in Europe. He is still revered and his family home, up on a slope overlooking the river, is definitely worth a visit. State owned then, it was nevertheless just a beautiful and warm family home. The village I believe is Bad Hoffen, as story book attractive as anything anyone might imagine.

It was on this trip that I had another of those wonderfully warming experiences in this a bit tourist undertravelled Germany. I had booked a room at the start, in Cologne, not knowing as always what I would be getting. (In my many travels I often had to hotel shop after arriving somewhere. Many first days were that way - booking unknown can make for much walking around trying to find what you might be happy with. Wait until you read Geneva later.)

At any rate, even at about 3 pm as I remember it, my room was not ready. It was a small hotel but with its own restaurant. A husband and wife owner team.

I asked might I have lunch? The husband said well the dining room is closed right now, between meals, but he called to his wife in German. She said something about dinner, I wasn't sure what. So…he invited me to have a beer and since his wife was just preparing dinner I might be the first to enjoy if I could wait maybe 20 minutes. The beer was one of the best - all in Germany are not - and I had a very fresh schnitzel and equally fresh vegetables.

I don't want to make too much of this but it was a special touch and not at all necessary. The invitation for the beer on the house and the just done home cooked dinner.

We also, for you taxpayers, squeezed in a few business things on the visit. We checked on German coal mine reclamation regulations, hoping to glean a regulatory truth I might import and hand to my ho hum employer. We also popped east to the NATO storied town of Fulda whereat we dropped ourselves into a salt mine being used as a hazardous waste disposal site.

Salt mines are good for this, being dry and geologically stable. It was a bit exciting also. You zip down in a high speed mine shaft elevator, dump yourself into a hummer, keep your head low as instructed or risk losing it, and zoom off at speed in total darkness but for your headlamps. We braked hard, lights came one, and we found ourselves in a hazardous waste storage vault with a couple of people all primed to brief us. They finish, light outs, heads down, off we go. Repeat several times over. It was an impressive performance of German discipline and industrial management. Whatever one's predilection it was very impressive, the timing and overall organization. Almost dazzling in fact.

That mine ran for some 50 linear underground miles I believe we were told. Seems like a big number now, in retrospect. Maybe it was 50 miles of roads.

Whatever…it was very nice to come back to the surface. Amazing how some people earn a paycheck.

So enjoy Bonn, take a Rhine River cruise and see river villages, find a humongous Gothic cathedral somewhere, and drop yourself into a hazardous waste disposal mine, carefully.

An unusual jaunt in its variety.

Prague 2000; Once More is Just Fine and The Marsupial Tea Cup

Once again my job at EPA took me to Prague. In truth I paid for much of this travel in that EPA did not take kindly to civil serpents running off to Europe to give speeches at technical conferences. I got on my boss all the time about this but his stock answer was what can we learn from them in person that a few hours at the computer would not do. He was a real mixer. And a tower of research competence. But not to complain too much; EPA asked so little of me, got so little from so many others, and I made it to Europe whenever a conference showed up.

This particular circle of professionals, focusing on the horrible environmental problems in post Soviet eastern Europe, met in Prague, Warsaw and Budapest every two years. This broke my heart of course. In truth there was so very much to learn, and I got to visit places that were so important to me.

But I never made it to Budapest. Funding for this work was largely courtesy of the U.S. Congress and the Bush Administration cut it off before Budapest came my way.

This time I stayed across the Vltava river, in German the Moldau. Across from downtown Prague. This is the river of so many bridges and so many beautiful views I spoke of. And of Smetyna. Amazingly one can travel by boat from Prague to the U.S., or even Australia - imagine cruising through locks, the Elbe and from that great river north to the North Sea and on to anywhere. I'm sure many thousands have done it, booked tight each year. I did do a local cruise in a fast small boat just because I can't stay out of boats.

As you cross the river and begin to walk up, the look back at the city begins to take shape. Again, it's the best. The mix of river and architecture are superb from this walk. The walk gets steep but not too much so. As you look back you might wonder about the architecture - how much was spared and how much rebuilt? Prague had seen the ravages of two world wars. I'm still checking this out.

On that far side is the Prague Castle built in the ninth century. Not a castle in the tall turretted tourist sense but rather a huge set of buildings well worth seeing and the official residence of the President of the republic. I had first known of the castle during the presidency of the so highly regarded Vaclav Havel, a dissident writer turned immediate post communist internationalist and environmentally concerned statesman. Havel remains a beloved Czech figure.

It was on this trip that I found the so interesting tea cup. An ordinary coffee or tea cup except that it had built into its side a ceramic pocket for a tea bag. Lift your tea bag, squeeze it, and simply drop it on the side of the cup. No extra plate needed. I thought immediately...never seen these before, bet you could sell a million in the States. But I only bought one and never followed up. Might have been fun to establish the Tea Bag-Sided Tea Cup Company. Another super idea down the tubes. My entrepreneurial spirit had gotten lost somewhere. My son-in-law, tea only no coffee, now has the cup. (I want it back, Doug!!!)

And of course, with some people I met at the conference, I went searching for music again. Everywhere downtown young people are handing you one-pagers describing one concert or another. We were given one touting a terrific program in the old Jewish quarter, in what had been a synagogue or so it said. These four musicians turned out to be just the best and the hall, indeed a sanctuary before, had mementos of its religious past. Kind of a heavy experience, and so wonderful because of the music. Mozart, Beethoven and somebody else I don't recall.

I did Prague again in 2004, a quick visit off my Munich trip to be described later. But I can't say enough about it. For me it's the best one week visit in central Europe. And of course it's a great jumping off point for Vienna, Budapest or further south down to Venice or Trieste. Maybe a great idea…I'm only 73, today is my birthday as I write this, so plenty of time.

Or perhaps I'll do the boat trip Prague to Annapolis, Maryland where I live. With my marsupial cup.

THE BALTIC COAST OF GERMANY - 2001: SIMPLY PERSONAL NOT SPECIAL

I love the sea. In truth I need water close by. I've tried the mountains and even our southwestern deserts. I owned a ski lodge and ski area restaurant, a blast if one wishes to lose money fast, and I served for four years in the army at Ft. Bliss and the White Sands Missile Range, posts that were little but desert. For good reason too, firing huge antiaircraft missiles made sense only if not too many people were about.

But I was raised on the sea, in a town actually part of New York City but with its own very clear cut coastal flavor...the Rockaway Beach I mentioned earlier. My parents' house was two and a half blocks from the Atlantic Ocean, and about one and a half from Jamaica Bay on the other side. I recall during one hurricane we had water deep in the streets, and in our basement - the ocean and bay had met outside. I even remember the beach fortified during WW II.

As a boy and right through my early teens I felt that ocean was mine. I was there just about every day, swimming and fishing, from May until September. Visitors from Brooklyn or elsewhere in the steaming hot city, but for a few girls I came to know later, were not welcome at my beach. In fact we had very tight parking regulations; it was almost a private beach. And a very beautiful one, as are so many on the south shore of Long Island.

In my continuing and truly fruitless search to learn Berlin, into which I had flown so many times, I found that after a few days and no guide or friend living there, this huge so complex city with its past of rich culture and so much war and tragedy just depressed me. Here I was again but I had to get out. This is a problem til this day; I want to come to know Berlin but don't how to go about it. It may be that both my time and Berlin's are in the past, a not very happy thought.

And so it was, in 2001, after another such half hearted attempt at cruising Berlin alone - this was my mistake of course - I should have planned this and gotten help - I just decided to get out of town. There was the north, the Baltic, only a couple or three hours drive, and loaded with beaches.

It was summer also, beach time for sure.

I headed north for Rostock, a small city noted for its Hanseatic heritage, and formerly within the Soviet occupied zone. Rostock had been a very important seaport in the German Democratic Republic, but with reunification began to lose out to its western German competition. It had been heavily bombed in WW II but was rebuilt of course.

Up that way also, but I wasn't exactly sure where, was Peenemunde, the site of the testing of the V2 rockets - the rockets that had they been available a few years earlier might have had a dramatic effect on the ability of Britain to ward off a German land attack, British navy notwithstanding. V2s carried 2000 pounds of explosive, flew at some 3500 miles per hour and reached London in under 10 seconds. Some 1000 reached London even as Germany was collapsing.

It's worth noting here that much of what is written about Chamberlain's caving in at Munich to Hitler's demands for the Czech Sudetenland, with Chamberlain thereby achieving his "peace in our time", fails to take into account the so rapid pace at which weapons of immense destructive capability were being developed just then...and into the atomic bomb 1940s.

Think for a moment. If Hitler and possibly the Japanese had been forestalled for even as little as five years, by dint of a tougher Allied stand against Hitler's easy expansion through central Europe, or by allowing the Japanese more of the oil they so desperately sought…if global war had been postponed perhaps five years…which side might have had the atomic bomb sooner? The late arrival of the V2s, the world's first ballistic missile rockets, pales in its significance next to this notion.

So of course…wars might sometimes have to be fought earlier rather than later. Not a new idea. While our worst president ever screwed it up royally, Neville Chamberlain maybe got it right. Unknowingly. Still, his nickname was Pinhead.

I've really digressed in this piece. New York beaches, deserts, rockets, Chamberlain. Grand strategy. Excuse. It all popped in.

But to the beach.

These Baltic beaches were so remindful of my own on Long Island but for the absence of the long ocean swells. This part of the north German coast looked almost straight north across at Denmark. I was looking out at in effect at the southwestern Baltic, extending southwest to northeast. There was no long reach that would allow substantial swells and every day long waves. At least that was how I saw it; I know there can be quite stormy days and difficult seas.

The water was cold but no matter to the German bathers. Many were nude, no big deal at all. Very wide comfortable sand beaches and all the beautiful grasses whose names I don't ever bother to learn.

And a great very beautiful small hotel the name of which I still recall in my mind - the Bodestrand in one of the "Munde" - Trave, Peene or Warner. The restaurant was as pretty as any I've seen anywhere. Soft blues with sea views.

What topped it off for me were the two dogs at the hotel. That's me as you know. They were the owner's, two big Rhodesian Ridgebacks (or maybe one was a Doberman I don't really recall). Sleeping near the front desk. I befriended them as always; I'm a getter downer.

As I was bringing my luggage out to my car the owners sent these two protectors out to me to say goodbye. They came to the car and did as bid…many wags and licks from these couple of hundred pounds of teeth and watchfulness. Nice, for me.

Well, I didn't say much about the coast. But I did say a lot. Hope it was ok.

POZNAN 2002 - THE SO EMOTIONAL VISIT -
A WELCOME HOME
FROM THE POLISH ARMY COLONEL

I had another good friend in Poznan, a man about the age of my older children, about 42 at the time. I've mentioned him earlier - Walery Lach - the youthful professor of marketing when marketing did not exist, under Communism. I still wonder how in the world college level teachers at that mind numbing time might stand before students craving knowledge and fake an entire semester. I've taught economics, and marketing, and both are tough enough when you have substance. Is it easier when you don't? When you teach nothing? I can't figure this at all.

Nice job Walery had. I hope it paid. It didn't but it was a job.

Years ago a close relative once tried to make some aspects of Communism sound a bit appealing, wondering why it had not caught on. The discussion never got to killings and gulags. I simply asked if the notion of not being able to read what one might wish to read was a good idea. She backed off fast.

Walery's family then did not include the new little boy, Adam, who came along later to be the brother of 15 year old Szymon. It was Walery, his wife Beata, his son Szymon, and his dad Mateusz (for Matthew).

His dad was an interesting guy. Maybe ten years my senior. About 5 foot 3 or 4, stocky, always dressed immaculately; tie, jacket the whole bit. I was staying with Walery and his family and I always sat near the dad at meals.

We could not speak, had no common language, but I guess the idea of age made some sense. And Walery knew of my early Pentagon background.

Ready now?

This almost 80 year old had 60 years earlier served in the Soviet Army, rising to a colonel of Polish tank forces, fighting the invading Germans. He had escaped east, fleeing the Germans as did so many Poles. If you are interested in how some of this played out read Joseph Davies "Short History of Poland", a masterpiece by the preeminent English scholar. Poland has been such a happy place, with powerful invaders bursting through every few years. Count your blessings again.

And he was a Polish Jew. A Jew fleeing to the Soviet Union, a far better place to be if you can grasp that, just then for sure. He had married a Muscovite, so Russia was not new to him.

Mateusz, as I said, rose to be a full colonel in the Polish army, a tank regimental commander, under the Soviet Marshall Rokossovski who commanded a full army of Poles fighting Hitler. By coincidence Rokossovski was himself of Polish origins. A memorial had been planned and built honoring Mateusz' regiment, but under Gomulka, with his policies of anti-Semitism, the Soviets then re-discovered his religion and the project cancelled. Nice, huh?

Mateusz and I had been together and sat near a few times. We watched one another. Both of us curious I guess. I knew of his albums of WW II pictures but had never seen them. I wanted to and asked Walery to ask him. He almost burst with smiles, we would do so.

After dinner we moved to the living room and grabbed a corner with two chairs. Album after album, with me not understanding him but relating pretty well to the photographs. I knew the war well, from all my studies and years of interest. Walery came by to see how we were doing.

(At this point as I write I'm beginning to choke a bit. Know that. You'll soon see why. It always happens. I guess I'm not so very tough.)

I asked Walery if his dad knew I was Jewish. He said no. I said tell him. He did.

The 80 year old 5'3" tank commander jumped to his feet and held out his arms to me. I stood and he embraced me and spoke in Polish.

Walery told me what his dad said.

He said to me…welcome home.

This man who had lost his own home and family and would have given his life said to this American Jew who knew no such joys…welcome home. As I've said, I'm not at all religious. But guess what?

I haven't told this story in years. It still moves me as much as anything I've ever known.

Walery - I owe you for bringing this to me.

Krakow 2003 - A Special City and Maybe the Best Special City of All

This is a glorious and captivating city. It is a city of under a million yet draws seven million visitors each year.

Krakow sits just north of the Carpathians in south central Poland. It is on the upper Wisla, the Vistula, River - the river that almost bisects Poland and runs all the way up to the Baltic Sea. It is just east and down river of the heavily industrial region centered near Katowice and as a result the river and the region bore the ravages of rampant Communist time pollution. Heavy metals in particular scarred the river bed. This is an extremely difficult problem to clean up. Thank you Soviet Union. Thanks too Cold War.

It is a city over 1000 years old and considered by many to be the historical capital of independent Poland. It was named a European City of Culture in 2000. It has 28 museums and art galleries. The city supports 18 universities and some 170,000 students. It is or was home to two Nobel prize winners, Wislawa Szymborska and Czeslaw Milosz. (The numbers above were taken from the free on-line *Wikipedia* encyclopedia.)

Some 45 minutes west by bus is the Polish town of Oswiecim. Have you not heard of Oswiecim? It also goes by another name - Auschwitz. Birkenau is just outside of town. Auschwitz-Birkenau. Yes I did go and I'll get to that.

Nearby also was another concentration camp - Plaszow - not seen by me.

I had done a little homework. I knew of the old town and old market - all major Polish cities I knew had their Stary Miasto and Stary Rynek. I knew it had a concert hall;

again all cities I'd known did. It had the huge Royal Castle on Wawel Hill, and it was close to Zakopane, in the Tatra mountains, a ski resort to the south. Krakow was storied also in my studies of WW II, being one of Hitler's early targets in the south just north of the Czech border as he rushed to isolate Warsaw.

Schindler's List, a winner of so many awards, was filmed in Krakow. Krakow had when I visited a small Jewish community and memorial in Kazimierz the former Jewish section. How small a community now I'm not sure: I think I was told about 200. What was left or re-begun.

Krakow was a winter trip. It was cold. First time I'd ever sat in a small plane and watched the de-icing tower spray us down. The small planes were the flights over the mountains to and from Munich. I'd not thought of it ever before but I mean to tell you it was comforting watching this get done.

LOT Polish Airlines, by the way, has an enviable safety record, and - important fact of no consequence except to me - Polish pilots in the RAF accounted for a very high percentage of kills of German aircraft during the Battle of Britain. Was it 20%? Whatever, I always feel comfortable on LOT. I like small aircraft in general.

But back to Krakow.

The architecture jumps out at you in places - a mix of gothic and renaissance. It can be breathtaking. I recall the gothic church in the Stary Rynek, St. Mary's. It is of the 14th century and shelters the most impressive ever and very tall wooden altar. There is a legend associated with this church, of a melody played every hour on trumpet but each time cut off unexpectedly. It seems that in the 13th century a guard playing to warn of Tatar attack was killed and his warning stilled.

I also remember in the Stary Rynek one restaurant in particular; I think it was called Hawelka but I'm not sure. Warm, quiet, modest in price, wonderful servers, and looking out on as pretty a market square as one can imagine. Polish food? Eastern European food? Pierogi and kielbasa are the least of it. Best you not try any.

Another restaurant sticks in my mind. Wandering down some side street after visiting the castle, I spied a walk-down restaurant. After Prague I became a sucker for these; they always seemed to get better the further underground they were. This one was decorated to be Ukrainian, Ukraine not being so very far away. For me it was a fairy tale of sight.

The food was spectacular. Ukrainian food, as we confirmed later in Moscow, tends to be abundant, uniquely for me flavorful and so very attractive as presented. I recall the incredible triangular dumplings (galushky), the different and so fresh salads, and the many appetizers and main courses that just lit me up as I read of them. I did no vodka then but made up for it in Moscow as you'll see later if you read on. Many varieties and all delicious.

The old market just hummed in the evening, cold as it was the many shops and stalls were open late, music was all about, and stands of hot grilled kielbasa and much more were grabbing at me…quite successfully. I was in food heaven.

Are you getting the message about this city?

The Jewish district, Kazimierz, is tiny now, a few blocks at best. Not a particularly nice neighborhood but I was told was being rebuilt with shops and cafés coming. There were signs to the memorial. I forget whether it had been a place of worship but now it was a few rooms with films of old Krakow and Krakow under the Nazis being shown. Empty but for me, two employees, and a couple visiting. I walked in, said hello and was directed to the few simple exhibits. I thanked them and walked past to see everything. I was called back.

My big mistake. They wore skull caps. I never did even here in the States. You all know how I feel about oversold in your face religion in today's so violent world.

The mistake was this was not today's world. I was a fool to not see this. I put on a skull cap. A film and as always with my roots…very moving exhibits.

You want something about Oswiecim? About Auschwitz? Ok.

What I recount below of Auschwitz is from memory. In fact, as I said before, all of what I've written is from memory, but for where I've noted otherwise. I took no notes on my trips. Please excuse an error or two.

Don't bother about the Holocaust Museum. Save a few bucks, fly to Krakow, enjoy this city of unparalleled legend, beauty and tradition…and take a bus ride.

A bus ride from beauty to bestiality.

You pull in at the base camp, the red bricked administration buildings. Maybe a couple of dozen, I forget, surrounded by barbed wire, watch towers, Arbeit Macht Frei, the whole bit. The whole horrifying bit. You get the speech, from a Pole who dutifully does this to make a living. You see pictures of all the early inmates, all Polish non-Jews (the so-threatening intelligentsia) and you see huge windowed displays of hair, teeth, and shoes. You are told of and shown interrogation and torture areas and rooms. You are shown the outside execution wall. Better, perhaps by far, to be shot than to be placed in the detention cell...I think it was about 2' x 2' x 4'...too small to stand - or to sit. For hours and days.

Is that enough of Auschwitz? Let's go to Birkenau. Back to the bus and a short ride...a kilometer or two.

You debark at the adjoining administration buildings, two small buildings separated by the incoming single train track. One track, the trains entering full and reversing empty. On entering a few passengers were culled out for some duty or other, the rest waived on to the...stables.

You climb a few stairs, one or two flights, and look out over acres and acres of these stable-like structures, with three empty spaces where the ovens were. As I recall you look out a half mile or so. Acres and acres of now decrepit wooden stables in which inmates were stacked awaiting death.

It was as I said winter. I'd wanted to see Auschwitz in winter. I did.

Don't let these final words turn you off. Visit Krakow for sure.

Warsaw to Poznan - 2004; A Very Bittersweet Taste of Life Past and Present

This was indeed another trip for emotion. Not as much so as my welcome home by the Jewish Polish colonel or the entire Krakow experience but still a visit to be remembered. Mary shared all of this one with me. This was her first visit to Warsaw.

We began with yet another professional meeting. Coal combustion in power plants is every inch the issue in Europe as here. In eastern Europe, however, air and ash disposal pollution issues still dwarf our own; again the legacy of mindless Communist times. Still progress is being made.

Sadly, this overt domination once by Soviet Russia has now transformed itself into almost total yet more subtle dependence on Russia for gas and oil. An international political nightmare of unknown future implication for regional relationships…and regional peace.

Our conference was as always just a pleasure. It was hosted by a friend of mine, Tomasz Szczygielski, a Pole who had made himself a name in re-using the many tons of coal ash produced by power plants. Tomek arranged a Chopin concert in a palatial museum, for all 100 or so of us, and then a dinner at a wonderful old town restaurant, once again inside the Stary Rynek, the old market.

We sat at tables of eight or ten. The centers of each table as we began were fully covered, I mean fully covered, with platters of very fresh salads, and wonderful meats and fish. The best of Polish breads, and these are the best in

Europe for my money, were everywhere. Hardly any space existed for our own plates.

These salads did not leave. They were not "taken out of our way" - they stayed and we so enjoyed the play back and forth of the foods. There were the usual soups including a borscht that non-borscht people would love, and appetizers. Pierogi of course but much more, followed by the main course choices. It was a fine eating establishment by any mark, west or east. Each entree was fresh and hot, not easy for 100 people, and of the best spices and flavors. I have no idea what all these taste sensations were; I just enjoyed so incredibly much. It was not until Moscow, coming up later, that Mary and I again saw a feast like this one. In Moscow there were two such!

Also, vodkas. Some had some. Maybe a little.

Up river, the Wisla or Vistula again, just a few miles is the village of Kazimierz, same name as the section of Krakow of which I spoke. A very picturesque town, overlooking the river, and of course a new town…some 1000 years old. As you might suspect from seeing his name so often, Kazimierz had a following - He was King Casimir the Just. They all were Just, Bold, Wise or something else modest. I'm not going to tell you too much of this town - just go and Google it up. Check the pictures. It's but a short tour bus ride from Warsaw and well worth it.

Again, this time with Walery Lach as our guide, we did the historical monuments. I think the one that moved Mary the most was the Umschlagplatz; we were after all standing on the exact spot where so many had been shipped to their deaths at Treblinka. Mary's roots are not too dissimilar to mine but hers include some Ukrainian Jewish.

How many times have I thought…we don't get to pick our forebears; we can only accept and explore what we are. Imagine if we were horribly poor Tutsi?

With Mary I shopped. We walked Polish streets and malls or near malls. Poland, or at least Warsaw, has come to the modern world. Maybe not upper Madison Avenue everywhere but good quality goods everywhere. Of course much traffic. Way to go, Poland. About time. And even New York is not everywhere upper Madison Avenue. We also found any number of wonderful little coffee and pastry shops. All of this I should add is very close to the main railway station, as I said called the Warsaw Centralna, and nice big city walking.

My good friend Walery, he of the colonel dad of whom I told you, worked in Warsaw then. He drove to and from Poznan, some four hours, weekends. He would drive us to Poznan. Lucky us, free ride.

Walery never got below about 90 miles per hour, 140 km or more. This is not uncommon on good German roads but Polish back country two laners? Walery, good buddy…trees? Cars? Trucks? Bikes? Villages? Children? Did you notice any in the blur?

Once we approached a sort of parked bus on our right and an oncoming speck, an old woman it turned out, on a bike. He timed it such, without slowing, so that we had a full six inches, 13 centimeters maybe, on each side. Plenty of room he said, why slow. He and I had a few words later, figured I should tell him he had a young family.

But he did something very special for us. We detoured north. He wouldn't tell us why.

He stopped with nothing showing at the road side. He said as he often did in impatience...c'mon. We walked a few steps across the road and into the open grassy area maybe 20 yards, I don't recall. But back a little ways.

There we found a small sign. This was Chelmno, the death site where, it said, 400,000 Jews had been put to death by carbon monoxide in closed trucks. That's a big number, if I remember it right. In trucks. Maybe only 200,000? Add these to all the rest.

One more unexplained detour. We slowed. For this alone we were thankful. Next we knew we were in a village that might have been 100 years old, a classic in appearance schtetl. Very narrow dirt road, small wooden almost crude huts right at our car doors. Plants in every window. Walery said it was legit, but now Poles lived in it. This was surreal. Would it not have been destroyed and changed? He said no. I wonder.

This was fun in Warsaw and excitement, and then suspense after that. Yes, another death camp.

Please remember, as I've said, I have legitimate questions about religion as do so many. But if you want to see how delightful it has been to so many, Jew and Christian alike, have a go at parts of Poland. You'll likely come away asking why God ever bothered with several different religions. If there is but one God why so many religions? Perhaps a well thought out prank?

MUNICH - 2004; MAD LUDWIG
YOU DID GOOD

I'd not done much in southern Germany, not in Bavaria nor yet in the west, Wurttemburg for instance, to be described a little later.

What does Munich have? Only Everything.

Munich is storied for legendary mad kings, for castles, for beer, BMWs, for the nearness of astounding mountains, even for Hitler's early years. Dachau, not visited my me, a camp of some 170 locations and even extending south to Austria is but a half hour ride to the west.

Flying in is the best compared to Frankfurt. Frankfurt's airport is a busy confused mess, right up there with JFK. Munich's is new, 1992, very clean and easily navigated. If you have a choice you don't - pick Munich. As with Frankfurt, no problem getting a train to downtown as I recall maybe 30 minutes away. This is a big city, an internationally attractive tourist city. And it offers many out of town sights even Austria so close by to chase down. It takes some planning

This is a location, a region, of astounding sights.

I had no hotel when I arrived but within an hour I had checked out many by walking near the train station and had my plenty good enough three star right in center city. This was often my way, even though being tired from the flight may make this not for everyone.

But try it. It only hurts that first day. And the more hotels you look at the better the sleeping in the one you do select. No matter how awful. Collapse.

A wonderful central shopping area, the Marienplatz. Pre just Christmas!! No cars of course, just shops and blow your mind coffee houses. Very close to that same central train station and even the Munich Philharmonic. At the Philharmonic I caught the Irish pianist Barry Douglas whom I knew from his press but had not ever heard play. A dramatic modern Philharmonic hall.

One quick first impression of Munich, airport and symphony hall - is all so newly built?

Beer halls if you're so inclined. Pretty dull actually to look at, long rows of tables undoubtedly noisier in October than when I visited in December. You've got to be a little careful with German beer, it isn't all great. Same as here of course. Ask for what you want, a Pils or a dark whatever. They very much vary by taste and region.

Munich, like Heidelberg and so many German cities, is a renowned university town. I don't mean to overplay this culture and heritage business, only to point out to those who may care that virtually everywhere one travels in Germany a sense of centuries old culture is all about. You almost travel back in time, as much so as in France or anywhere I've been. I love it. Thank you Old Europe.

And in Munich...the seemingly so new mixes easily with the centuries old.

Munich also has a rebuilt synagogue and Jewish community, bearing this point out. Last I looked Germany had some 100,000 Jews, compared to Poland's uncountable 10,000 or so and over 500,000 in France. Germany as I've said defies any early 21st century political stereotyping.

Germany is multi-faced, Poland not at all so. I noted this before - what a change over, what, three decades? Total reversal from pre WW II of course. France of course is a kaleidoscope of skin colors. I mention this is in speaking of Strasbourg later.

Why these changes? Need we wars for this? Or just religion? Economic opportunity? Immigration stresses? Why?

I popped down to Berchtesgaden then and to Austria...Salzburg. It's so easy to say it now but this is an extraordinary little trip , maybe 100 kilometers south, with not to be believed castles and mountains. I mean...an hour or so on the best roads imaginable.

Berchtesgaden was Hitler's mountain retreat and I'd wondered for so long how could this be - how could that creature appreciate beauty? But he did of course, he even painted. Is this possible? Now it's just a town of some 7000 in the Bavarian Alps and only 30 km from Salzburg.

Mount Watzman, the third highest in Germany, may be found there. In the 1920s much of the area was simply appropriated by the Nazis. The remnants of the Nazi homes have been long since demolished but the Eagle's Nest, a gift to Hitler on his birthday in 1939, I believe, still is preserved.

I'm not recommending a visit to Berchtesgaden unless you happen to be the WW II buff I am. Everything else along the way though makes it a natural stop.

Now for Ludwig, Ludwig the second. The first was a dud.

This guy built the most beautiful castles in Europe. This guy also had relationships with many men, and gee so oddly never produced an heir. This guy was much beloved at the time, if one is to believe what is now written - he kept Bavaria peaceful although he did sell out to Bismarck and he enjoyed mixing with common folk but avoided parties - my kind of guy with the parties (only). Still he was a buddy of Wagner. Just go look at these castles built by him; they are for real...tall and reaching for the sky.

Story book real castles. You don't need to go in; I didn't. But see them.

When he died he was declared insane. Paranoid schizophrenia in today's terms. I think we have worse, measured against impact on world affairs, not yet anointed as I write.

Salzburg? If you know Mozart, or just ski, you know this town. Big time Austria ski town complete with its own airport and even an S-Bahn system. The ski mountains to the south of the city are where one goes, the city itself being only some 400 meters elevation. This is a town ski or not, that has it all, to include enough baroque architecture to last you some time.

Ok. Munich itself.

But for buildings of newness no real impressions here. I met few people who stick in my mind. It's a hustling apparently well to do BMW town with a ton of things to see and do in and around within an hour so.

But thanks to you Mad Ludwig for setting up shop here. You were one colorful dude.

Go visit this whole scene. Take at least a week.

Frankfurt, Beautiful Heidelberg, First Touch of the Black Forest, and Pickpocketing Paris Style - 2004

I've landed at Frankfurt more times than anyone should. I mean it's a monster airport. I've aborted landings there and even suffered one near miss in the air. Right next door is the huge U.S. base, still, at Rheine Main. Still in all everything seems to work pretty well, if you don't mind long walks and long lines but as I said use Munich if you can or just grab a quick connecting flight after going up and down stairs five times.

But Frankfurt was one of my father's parents' towns, his father I think. (The other was Hamburg to which I've not yet been). I had searched down the address he had given me, years ago when he was lucid, on my first trip way back in 1971. Frankfurt was quite rebuilt even back then and where he pointed me stood a new house. There I stood next to the house, in 1971, me and my grandparents' address - but the photo did nothing for my father. I was not sure whether it had been just disinterest or his early failing.

Frankfurt like Berlin always intimidated me. Huge, with so many secrets I'd never uncover, and so much too up to date now to be of interest to me. A few times I had overnighted here while awaiting a flight but that was it. But at least this time I zipped into town on the train.

Trains. Need I say much about trains in Germany? I've now done the train many times and it's just fun. Reliable, well signed, comfortable, frequent, everything you've heard about. Second class is fine and don't even bother with a seat assigned unless the station agent says to do it because of expected crowding up the line. Sit back and relax, which is so fine after the air travel.

Just across from the air terminal - the entire humongous airport - is the Frankfurt Flughafen train station. From there to anywhere in Europe sooner or later. But it is a hike and be prepared to sit and await your train. I would just unwind waiting and knowing soon a town and my luxurious three star hotel would show up.

As I said just above, one time I grabbed a commuter train from the airport into downtown Frankfurt. I'd read about a small museum, displaying the story of the history of Frankfurt's Jewish community and from my map a nice walk in town. It turned out to be just as billed - a couple of floors of drawings and pictures depicting local life spanning as I recall five hundred years or more.

So, like Berlin, Frankfurt still eludes me. I feel disappointment but maybe since I seek impressions new modern cities should be as they are, way down my list.

Still - here come some impressions now.

Heidelberg is a place of sublime beauty and with it came my first taste of the Schwarzwald, the Black Forest. This is a town that just captures your senses...I mean it grabs you. Castle, old city, ancient university setting, glorious river, situated in hills...just beauty everywhere. I should admit I spent no time in the newer part of town, saw no reason to. Heidelberg simply knocks your socks off.

Heidelberg is but an hour or so by train south of Frankfurt. Easy autobahn car ride also, which I did because I was on my way again west, to see Isabelle's new home -

her own first home - east of Paris. A town of 140,000 that sees over 3 million visitors each year, it sits on the River Neckar, across from a broad and extended hillside embracing Philosopher's Walk, a long, spectacular walk high up overlooking the river. The university dates back to the 1300's and its presence in the old town is just enchanting. The castle sits just behind and to the side of the university. All of this, including Philosopher's Walk across the Alte Brucke, the old bridge, is easy and delightful walking. Coffee shops whenever you want one of course, but my most felt impression was simply of timeless beauty and civilization.

Heidelberg is well said to be one of the most beautiful cities in Germany. Stay in the Old Town of course, and near the Alte Brucke unless business compels you to be elsewhere.

The city is in the north of Baden-Wurttemberg, the southwesternmost of German states and bordering France and Switzerland. Terrible location, huh? Later I'll speak of Baden-Wurttemberg, as I describe my visit deeper into the so incredibly pretty Black Forest.

Ok? Visit Heidelberg and stay in the Altstadt. Prepare to lower your blood pressure and breathe beauty.

But now…what the hell…off to Paris again and Isabelle. Drive west, via Saarbrucken, Metz and the A4 to Paris.

Isabelle had done it finally, She'd purchased her own home. This still young woman, by my counting, the same age as my oldest, taught school and did not have a ton of money at her disposal. So we were all so happy for her; she did it! Her own home after years of renting.

It lay about a 40 minute drive east of Paris, in a hamlet called Le Fahy, near Pommeuse.

What she did not tell me was that the exit one takes driving from Paris did not exist driving west, toward Paris, as I was. Same problem as my first drive to her earlier home. Exit? What exit? So I got to make many French u-turns and pay many small tolls. Oh well. She laughed it off as before. Dumb American tourist. Isa…did you do this purposely? Well done if so.

No sign help of course but after an hour of countryside sightseeing a very kind young Frenchman actually got in his car and escorted me. A straight shot from another village, called Faremoutiers, as he showed me. Faremoutiers itself was interesting; very tight and silent and the site of a monastery.

Isabelle's new home was hardly new. Just enchanting. Surrounded by a high hedge, now removed she says, it was then barely visible from the road. It was alone on the edge of a broad meadow, but just across and down the street were many neighbors and many animals. Zephyr, her very male cat, had a sweet deal…acres of fresh food on the hoof to bring home. Which he often did.

Isa had a plan and it was unfolding. She had already re-done the kitchen and dining room and the upstairs was fine. I'm not sure what else she had in mind, but with her highly flavored artistic flair and way of getting help from friends I suspect this countryside home is on its way to becoming a jewel.

Of course we did Paris again. It may bore her but, I'm happy to say, not me. Not ever I'm sure. I think this was the time I took a Seine cruise, a simple joy. But driving within the city itself is not difficult. Just get a good city map.

It was also the time I was seriously pickpocketed. It was a day of a typical French Metro strike but allowing any train engineer to operate a train if he wishes. Entrepreneurship at its finest.

Here's how it works. Strike is announced. Pickpockets, according to most distasteful rumor, all from southeastern Europe, telephone favorite train operator. Offer 50% if he runs a train. Trains are jammed beyond belief because so few operate. You make many friends very close up and personal. A few live in your pockets. Wham bam done.

True?

But I wouldn't trade a moment of this entire trip. Lost only a few euros. Now I carry all money and cards in a breast pocket. Took me too damn long to get smart.

MOSCOW 2005 - THE AIR SHOW, THE METRO, NO EVIDENCE OF ANYTHING DONE RIGHT, TWO INCREDIBLE FEASTS

Moscow, my first visit, was a big pain.

It was worth it because of the city it is - its place in world affairs and the feel it gives you even now for how far apart peoples truly are. Peoples in this case who should be closer in every way. Russian peoples, and we and them. You simply feel tenseness, hardness.

I wonder why I have so much to say of this visit? I really was not comfortable in this city of so much force in history. Much was for reason of language, in that everywhere else I visit I can read and even speak a little. I'm talking to myself now, trying to understand a little better.

I found the whole scene terribly impersonal, and suggestive of a harsh life that might be so much happier, more casual and warmer. Is it just current politics? Might it also be that our values, perish the thought, are not really as closely tied as we might like? Decades, at least, of having original and creative thought stifled can make for powerful bureaucratics and a stoney-faced mind set. My strong impression for sure.

All during my Pentagon years the Moscow Air Show was the Mecca for NATO defense people and spies of all nations. How to get there and not get rounded up? I guess some did, but not me. Not my bag.

But now it was open to all. Assuming of course you would go through the nonsense Russian drill of getting an "invitation" to visit Russia so that you might spend some money there. Poor Russia. It lives, still, and worseningly so some would say, in a time past, where the dehumanizing mixes with a deep and rich culture crying so to be truly free, seen and shared.

What was our invitation? A hotel reservation did it. This is an invitation? Our visa guy went to the Russian embassy with this and like magic came the visa. Invitation? Don't they know this is laughable?

Off we went, Mary and I, through Zurich, over central Europe, and then Belarus the answer to our midwest Flyover. I guess maybe three people each year visit Belarus willingly. I might someday if they ever wise up. My mother's parents were Minsk if she remembered correctly.

We landed at Domodedovo Airport, looking to us like most any other big city airport but for all the redoing underway. (Of the airports we've sampled, Copenhagen is easily the most plush. Bring lots of money to Denmark.)

Now...where was Walery Lach? My Polish friend, an aircraft air show buff in spades and speaking Russian easily, was to meet us at the airport. I can get by with a few European languages, in airports and restaurants anyhow, but zero Russian and especially zero Cyrillic characters. Generally I'm quite comfortable traveling - don't even plan half my trips until I land - but Moscow no thanks. I did indeed want some help.

Well, of course, he was there. Right after passport control, customs and our bags, there he was. With a car. The first of our Moscow cars, this one a 1978 or so Fiat heap. How in the world did he get this car?

It's easy in Moscow; you don't take cabs you stand roadside and thumb. Cabs rip you off, these thumb guys you negotiate with. These guys give you a ride, forgetting about work, dinner or wherever they might have been headed, and make a few rubles.

Don't think for a second Moscow is easy. It's a huge strung out city with habits quite unlike what we know here. No real problem if you know the city or have friends, or know the language, but otherwise not a city to take lightly. I recall later starting to spill some cold coffee out of a taxi and the driver, who spoke some English, almost screaming at me that if that police car saw this we would either pay a huge bribe or all enjoy some jail time. Nice, huh?

I'd chosen a Marriott four or five star to be sure. We dropped off and settled in. This was good! Next - meet for the Air Show - then Red Square, the Kremlin and tourist stuff. I mean after all...this was Moscow...not be visited for the first time very often.

Air shows take lots of space, particularly in this time of supersonic fighters and huge transports. The Russian show for years was held out of town a ways, at a facility geared to handling thousands of people and dozens of aircraft. No problem getting there. Walery and a friend of his, Ilya Solomovskiye, chaperoned us. The Moscow metro with stations of superb art as reputed, then a train, then a crushing mob and the show grounds.

But then we, and particularly I, had a problem. Ours was just getting in. Maybe six entry gates for over 100,000 people, each with a security scan and possible frisk.

Me? Getting very nervous with this whole bit. I am, ah yes, almost 70 at this point and have a little less sway over things than I used to. I began to need a toilet. Jammed in can't hardly move, can't read signs, can't get separated and don't wish a wet afternoon. With a nod through Walery to Ilya I peeled off from the mob crush and headed back toward the park entry where there appeared to be what I needed. A big whew. And Ilya bless his Russian caring waited for me back at the security gate.

No problem once inside. The crowd dispersed, toilets where you needed them, and a wonderful show. The highlights for me were a Russian SU-35 I think it was taking off almost vertically after a very short take off run, and a U.S. F-15 whose pilot we met later. Also a vintage U.S. B-52, on the ground close up for all of Russia to see. No more cold war.

That evening came the first of the two most memorable meals of my sheltered life. We all met - Walery, his 15 year old son Szymon, along with Ilya's wife Natasha and their 25 year old delightfully pretty daughter Maria, or Masha, at a Ukrainian restaurant. Masha, with a major in merchandising and very fine English, had a job at Moscow's Satchi and Satchi. Course after course, vodka after vodka unlike any you usually see here. I'll speak more of such meals later when I tell of dinner at Ilya's home. Now all I'll say is it was a restaurant experience not to be believed and made so perfect by having such hosts.

But this was Moscow. We were there. So next day to the Kremlin and Red Square. Red Square from the many news films and TV always seemed large and so imposing. Not so at all. The Square itself is fed by gates and surrounding streets and the news shots of huge missiles, tanks, trucks and all filing through never showed the feed into the square itself. Very few of those frightening weapons were ever in the square at the same time. Super perspective camera work on the part of the propagandists.

The Kremlin views, with the many domes, are of course timeless and beautiful, And we had to do the Kremlin tour, never expecting the wholly unintentional and even depressing humor we were to find.

We picked up our tour guide, the next day, just outside the Kremlin itself. A youngish woman and attractive, with solid if halting English. She struggled it seemed to me; with her tour guide speech seemingly so canned she needed little more to earn her paycheck. Tour guides and even docents I've heard, in Ireland, Britain and elsewhere, were often more fun than the tour itself. But this lady was running on empty.

And so inside the Kremlin walls. Then a few stops.

First at a huge and two piece shattered church bell. I mean huge. Maybe two stories. A major chunk lay to one side, about the size of a pickup truck. In her workmanlike and accented English, our lady proceeded to tell us that this was built by "*skilled* Russian craftsmen in the whatever it was 17th century but *there is no evidence* that it was ever rung." Skilled craftsmen, but busted up, and never rung? Like displaying a royal toilet never flushed? No grin, no glimmer of I know it's funny from our guide. This badly broken, probably dropped, never used bell they were proud of? Surely it might now be repaired. Even rung.

Looking ahead we could see a cannon of maybe 20 inches diameter. A land, not battleship, cannon, the biggest of any type I'd ever seen. I think in the first and second world wars a few about this size were employed. But this was much older...as I recall maybe 19th century. Here's our guide - "This cannon was built by *skilled* Russian craftsmen in the 19th century. However *we have no evidence* that is was ever tested or fired". Poor lady. Again no smile, no nothing.

Skilled craftsmen? Skilled designers? Maybe a working model of anything, please?

The Russians do and did have skilled craftsmen. I'm sure we all in our small group thought why can't they display something that works in this…their Kremlin? Do not, ever, try to equate the Russian mind to something we can easily appreciate. It wasn't just language. Even if our so insightful president, with his deepest of feeling for other cultures, can read Vladimir Putin's soul.

Just across from us, maybe 30 meters, was allegedly President Putin's office, in an ordinary looking office building bordered by dozens of smaller also 19th century cannon.

Very impressive. I figured for sure Russian cannon that worked! Nope. All were captured from Napoleon. So much for skilled craftsmen.

My wife needed to see the various museums, and she was right in insisting. Particularly the one containing every carriage ever made in Russia, all two zillion of them, every piece of Catherine's jewelry and every horse saddle and bridle ever made in Russia. Or I thought, the universe. I mean…three hours of this?

Ok. Ok! Enough. I sat down. I was whipped. Next to me dropped, tired also, a young American. Very fit. Maybe 27. We talked. He said he was the pilot of the F-15 we had seen at the air show. Tom Cruise kind of there in Moscow. He was tired? So, do you get it, how dull 5000 saddles can be?

You probably know these guys are fit; I mean they make many professional athletes look like couch potatoes. This guy was tired? He was totally overdosed. I was thinking I'd prefer a prostate exam.

The Kremlin tour needs to shed something. Hours. Be prepared.

Ah, but now...

Walery told us Ilya and Natasha, although speaking no English at all, wanted us to come to their home for dinner. Our American world can really use a small dose of reality, current reality or past, in a cultural sense, and that was what we two so-sheltered Americans found in first trying to find and then visiting their home! It was just so much a turn on, in every way.

We had the address. It was far across Moscow. Imagine getting from the upper Bronx to somewhere across Brooklyn, speaking only Swahili. I'm quite serious. No public transport we understood and no taxis because it might cost $250 pay or else.

With the address written in both English and Cyrillic we did as told, we thumbed. Another 1978 or so car stopped for us, this time a Trabant or Lada. I forget which. Look them up. Kind of communist Yugos but worse. I showed the address and we agreed on a price.

Not much traffic then and maybe 40 minutes later he slowed and began to scan around. We were looking, Masha had told us, for a movie theater and whatever the street was. What she had not told us was that to us it would hardy be recognizable as a movie theater. A Crown multi-cinema it was not. A king of garage with a sign was what it was. But no Masha; and she said she would be there for us.

So there we were. Stuck on some way out Moscow street in who knew where, with a who knew at all driver getting anxious for his money and to be gone. No way to communicate and so surprisingly me needing a bathroom.

Miracles do happen. Our new young lady friend came running down the street. Saved from a night on the street or a double the price ride back to the hotel.

We had just one more culture surprise on the way in. Approaching the apartment building all was dark. And run down, I mean beat up, and not anywhere a young woman and older couple should be hanging around. At least in our minds. We of course said nothing. In Russia apartments were like gold for years.

We just picked our way carefully through the empty courtyard, entry way, lower level…all very dark really with no lighting at all. For Masha it was nothing, she'd grown up here. Quite the ordinary experience in parts of the world we never see. Elevator and up to the apartment.

Yep…some serious relief. A bathroom too, more relief.

But so much space, so many rooms. We entered a short hallway, a very small bedroom to the left, ahead a combination living room/dining room/bedroom, perhaps 10 by 14 feet, behind us a tiny kitchen, maybe five by five feet. One small bathroom. A few years back a boarder had the small bedroom. Now it was Masha's. This, as you know, is not an unusual eastern European apartment situation. For those who were lucky.

Ilya led us right away to the dining table set for six, we five and Igor, Masha's boyfriend just back from Denmark. We were simply dazzled. It was covered entirely with foods, and, as it turned out, only the first course.

Marinated meats, breads, fruits, salads, mushrooms, vegetables, vodkas, bottles of wines, soft drinks. I'm sure in trying to recall, Mary and I overlook a few things. After that, everything home made - borscht, a dish of cubed beef, mushrooms, onion, and spices all baked and served in individual bowls, pierogi Russian style, and finally desserts sweet and wonderful. The table was never empty, never cleared. Just filled again and again. Again, the kitchen was five feet by five feet. Tiny refrigerator, no freezer. What do you think, America?

So how was Moscow? Of course go. Just plan it carefully.

2006 - IN THE STORYBOOK PRETTY BLACK FOREST AND ON TO STRASBOURG

As I said earlier in telling the dark truth about Texas, this part of Germany is my favorite. It isn't very big, sitting in the far south and west on the French/Swiss border, bordering French Alsace, and is immediately captivating. It runs, a kind of strip, north and south in the southwest of Baden-Wurttemberg.

Never have I seen so many enchanting towns, set into rolling green hills, each town with its eye appealing small hotels, restaurants and shops. Travel is so, so difficult -

regional trains, a sort of light rail, incredibly on time, and busses - just run around all the time. Some hotels, I was told, give you free bus tickets. Later, in getting to Strasbourg, I proved this out.

The Alps just ran out of push up here and left mankind a taste of gentle visual grace. What an incredible place to live, even with wet and chilly winters, it must be. I didn't really check the local economy; I saw lots of logging operations and the many clock shops, but I can't speak to how to make money. I did see people who looked, to my tourist eye, happy with their lot in life. The hills, remindful of our beautiful Blue Ridge in Virginia, have been acid rain damaged but seemed ok to my eye. The logging at least now, I was told, is carefully controlled. Careful culling only. I hope so. Typically Germany gets this stuff done right well ahead of the U.S.

So what do I say? I say visit this part of earth heaven and do it with some time to spare. Get a car, as I did, to wander. To Strasbourg I did the bus just to avoid traffic and parking. And yes…if you must wander further…zip to more of France, or Switzerland all of about an hour or less away.

Strasbourg is so close and is a city with a wonderfully appealing multi-racial culture.

Amazing what a simple walk across a border can do. From what I saw in Germany, a white skinned part of Germany unlike so many parts of the north I saw, immediately in France every skin shading from white up though cream, brown and to the darkest of blacks. So exciting to see this, next door to the all white, in western Europe. (I'm not asserting there are no darker skin colors in the Schwarzwald. I don't know. I'm speaking of what hit me…the color differences.)

Another contrast was the so almost pristine cleanliness of this part of rural Germany with the mixture found in urban Strasbourg. This is a bit unfair, countryside against city, but again it was something I felt. As I walked through Strasbourg, I could sense the city struggle. Some streets were as well groomed and picked up as could be, others a mess. Cities are difficult of course. Towns are easier. No value judgement here, just my impressions - so France excuse me.

Strasbourg is another 1000 year old or so city. It sits on the River Ill, just off the Rheine, amidst many canals. I did the boat tour, in town, for my money rivaling the Paris Seine tour.

Alsace, so much a part of the French-German border struggle for so many years, is both French and German in its cultural roots. Architecture, restaurants, wines...a wonderful hodgepodge of both.

Now the city houses many of the European Union governing bodies, in office buildings that stick out almost like transplants from space in the midst of architecture of so many years past. Ok I suppose, but not for me. This leaps out at you on the boat tour.

This was an easy trip. A plane to Frankfurt, or Stuttgart if you wish, a car...and head southwest on those awful German roads. What came to my mind more than once was my wandering with my father in New England over 60 years ago.

Combine this with Heidelberg and have the time of your life. What a joy.

How about that for a vacation?

2006 - Geneva and Chamonix; The Red Light Hotel, the Strangest Train Station Ever and a Ski Town of Ski Towns

Mary and I wanted Geneva, wanted the lake and wanted the Alps. A decent package we thought.

We were so right.

Geneva is a another of those big cities, not as big as some, still a little hard to get to know as tourists. But we had a pretty good go at it. For some odd reason my wife was not content with the one star I had picked out and this made for some fun time. One and maybe two stars were always it for me, all the time; I thought she'd like the…thrill.

It was, I thought, a great hotel. Only a block and a half off the lake and quite inexpensive for Geneva, about $90 as I remember. The internet picture looked super. It didn't show the no elevator two long flights walk up, the breakfast of instant coffee and cold bread, the no telephone even for an emergency, no night clerk and the bathroom the size of an espresso maker. The shower did even have an overflow gutter. It overflowed to the floor. What else might one want? I thought, fine. Secretly at first, and then openly, another opinion was taking shape.

The next morning, as I happily slept off the jet blues, she disappeared. Gone hotel looking. She woke me and off we went. She had found a four star, even that being difficult this particular week. I said you gotta be kidding…four star in Geneva was $400 per night. $400!!!

So we walked and looked. For me this was always fun. I asked and met people and got to feel less a stranger wherever I was. Almost always, as I've said, I did not book ahead of time. I did the walk. But here it was a bit different. She loved walking but not my hotel picks.

We found a great upgrade, a three star, a nice room, nice café, nice people, phones, a TV of decent size. Everything. Always people around outside, also.

But she got people picky. And the lighting outside was too bright for her. Hot pinks and reds.

Geneva did indeed have a red light district. Maybe more than one, we never looked for another. But we were in the center of this one. Many quite friendly young people outside, both men and women. I liked it.

It was ok with Mary too, I thought, I mean this is why one travels. But the desk clerk made the fatal mistake - she told us not to worry the police were always right outside. For some reason this did not reassure Mary as it was meant to.

This hotel became instant history. She volunteered to pay a three day tab at the four star.

Did my scheming work or not?

A day later off to Chamonix. In the French Alps. Maybe three hours by train.

No zoom easy trip to Chamonix. Maybe because it's in France. I don't mean long, just a bit different.

First there is no direct train service from Cournavin, Geneva's main station. The tourist office told us to take a tram to the Eaux-Vives station, where we would catch the direct train. We did tram it, in rush hour, with our luggage. We guessed our way through a residential neighborhood, asking and finally found the station.

Station? Geneva? One of the world's wealthiest cities? This "station" was a dilapidated oversized garage, set inconspicuously into a mixed bag of light industrial or whatever buildings. Inside I found a woman cleaning; I showed her my ticket and she nodded. To a world class ski resort from a world class city? Huh?

We walked out to the *single* track. Overgrown with tall grasses and weeds, graffiti across the way, a man walking his dog on our track. Whoops? This was a scene from some wonderful film and we were living it.

Well. Right on time a two car 1910 or so train pulls in and a few hundred incoming commuters pile off. We were in the hands of the French SCNF, and off to the southeast we were, through France to the Alps. All four or five of us, replacing the horde of commuters. Through the Haute-Savoie, Upper Savoy, in France, the departmente adjoining Geneva to the southeast.

The train was great relaxing fun, a couple of changes and then up into the approaches to the Alps. Finally a gorgeous last few miles to Chamonix. As to Chamonix itself - it's hard to compare ski villages. We all have favorites This, though, was our first in the Alps and the so quickly rising slopes, sharp peaks and ski lifts - even the cable cars seemed to rise at 60 degree angles, to us, made this one special. The village itself would be the equal of anyone's most favored.

It was breathtaking. It was also September, a month of wonderful weather and few people.

And so back to Geneva. We had not done our lake cruises yet, something we both were looking forward to very much.

Lake Geneva, or Lac Leman to the locals, is just an ordinary oh so beautiful Alpine lake. It's remindful of New York's finger lakes; glacial, deep and cold, as I remember well from my college days. But no Alps surrounded the finger lakes. And no history of being the escape route for so many during one war or another is to be found in New York state.

We first did the boat to Lausanne, where I, the so cool traveler, managed to embarrass myself just perfectly. The right touch.

I commented to Mary, we plodding uphill from the dock in Lausanne, that, see, the girls are prettier, the shops so much more stylish, the cafés more authentic, the deals better than in Geneva. I allowed as how I was sooo glad we're in France again. Unfortunately we were not. Lausanne is proud to be Swiss. Lausanne? Brilliant me. I'd gotten my north and south shores mixed. The French shore is to the south.

I saw a Swiss sign of some kind. Girls, shops, deals… all got instantly less attractive.

To confirm my stupidity I had to ask at the train station, getting tickets back to Geneva, why he wanted Swiss francs. I mean we were in France, right? With a weird look the guy clued me in…again.

We did a second boat trip, the next day. We wanted to see the town of Yvoire, a medieval town, preserved for folks like us, and just an hour or so by boat away. Yep, French, the south shore of the lake, I had it now. Very touristy but at the cost of another great September cruise…do it. You'll feel 15th century.

I can truly imagine no more pleasant a region in which to live than the southwest of Germany, with nearby France and Switzerland. A few details remain to be worked out…like how possibly to do it. Sadly, no way for us now.

MAY 2007 - THE POLISH SEACOAST, BEAUTIFUL TOWNS AND SEALS

North central Poland was German for many years until the end of WWI when as part of President Wilson's fourteen point protocol for ending the war Germany was compelled to cede to Poland a corridor to the sea. Thus East Prussia came to be separated from Germany proper and the former German city of Danzig became the Polish Gdansk. When Germany attacked Poland in 1939 it did so from the west, the south…and the north; from this now separated but powerful East Prussia.

Germany claimed terrible injustices and crimes being committed by Poles against Germans in "Danzig" living under Polish rule. Yeah, right. Yet, in the eyes of many an ordinary German the loss of Danzig was but another of the odious terms forced on Germany by the Treaty of Versailles. Depends where one sits. It was among the easiest of Hitler's sells.

Much of this formerly German seacoast actually faces east, where the coast dips to a north south profile. This strip now contains the so famous port and shipyard of Gdansk, where WW II began and where Solidarity took root, the modern resort town of Sopot, and the new, only some 75 years old, port city of Gdynia. Solidarity, to remind you, was the first formal movement to find enough strength to challenge Soviet communism; and Lech Walesa, its leader, became Polish president. Walesa as I write has fallen somewhat in the eyes of his countrymen, but history will beyond doubt recognize him as a great moral and revolutionary political force.

So I set off for this coast, knowing I would find the sea I love so much but little knowing of the beauty and peace I would find.

Gdansk sprawls. It is splashed against the coast and the old town, the Stary Miasto, was different from those of the other Polish cities I knew. It too sprawled; it was not centered around an old market. But it is a beautiful tourist walk particularly with the various fingers of the Wisla, the Vistula, winding through in their final run to the sea. And German architecture vividly shows through still - there clearly is a bit of money.

Two locations in this town were a must for me - Westerplatte where the first known German WW II attack took place, and the Solidarity shipyard and museum. Except in their meaning, historically, both were unimpressive.

Westerplatte in 1939 was a small rounded peninsula facing east, embracing several ship mooring channels and stations, and housing an ammunition supply point. It was considered to be a Polish army transhipping station for both equipment and ammunition. Units of the Polish army and local police, totaling about 180 in all, were the guardians of this tiny post on Poland's sole outlet to the sea.

Amazingly, now in retrospect, on the day hostilities commenced, a German battlecruiser - descriptions vary of this ship - was moored in one of the inside channels. She was named the Schleswig-Holstein, a powerful ship for her time. She began WW II on September 1st with her shelling of the ammunition depot and close-by guard points. On September 3rd Britain and France declared war on Nazi Germany and total war was underway. The attack on Westerplatte grew into an assault from the land side as well, and by September 7th the few Poles left could do no more and surrendered.

This is a Polish historical site, as well it should be. It is crowned by a 25 meter stone tower commemorating the soldiers of this battle, with many of the original guard shacks still standing. As with so many such sites, even in the States but particularly in Europe (with Normandy being an exception), the emotion of the time is difficult to feel. At least for me it was, even with my sensing of those times. I wanted to be blown away. My God? WW II? A few shacks and one stone tower? But Poles perhaps feel things differently; their lives were - are - lives of day-to-day. How can we know what they lived?

There it was, a kind of seaside park…but where the horrific killing began.

I had a similar feeling in visiting the Gdansk shipyard where Walesa and his compatriots stood tall against the Soviets. I think it is worth repeating what I said before in these pages - that my observations suggested a Polish disgust and hatred of the Russians that really exceeded their fear of Germany. Germans came and went; Russians came and stayed, as some told me. Germans could think and one could

prepare; Russians carried clubs and said little. In that light
the Solidarity movement takes on an even more amazing
aura; the Poles stood firm and just a few historical years after
the shipyard worker strikes of 1970 and 1980 Communism
crumbled.

But the Solidarity monument location and museum
were a mess. Yes, the three towering crosses commemorating
the 1970 strikes are indeed impressive. But the Solidarity
museum, supposedly under remodeling when I visited, was
not only closed but a rundown eyesore. Even allowing for
a shortage of funds, and bureaucratic infighting, you would
think that so significant a political and moral event, and
location, would have long ago received priority attention
from both the Polish government and abroad. I hope soon
it will reopen and be accorded the station it deserves - as a
monument to the rescue of mankind from Communism.

The balance of this travel was standard stuff. Or
was it?

Wonderful and very inexpensive ferry boats to Sopot,
a beautiful resort town and long pier. A renowned hotel in
Sopot (the Grand Hotel, reminding me now of the Fairmont
Empress in Victoria, British Columbia). Great Baltic seafood.
And a visit to Hel.

Yes, Hel. This is the peninsula at the top of Poland,
extending southeast into the sea. It too brought memories.
It was narrow and very beachy, quite like in its emotional
feel, my boyhood home in Rockaway Beach, New York City.
The sea or bay, top and bottom, small homes and shops in
between. Gloriously peaceful in May, maybe a little cool

in winter. A seal rescue and visitor site stood virtually at quayside. Beautifully cared for and managed.

Of all my visits to Poland, this set of sea-related experiences was the most relaxed and most just pleasant. Does the sea do this? Of course it does. Maybe Poland is winding down for me. Maybe I'm winding down. But I tell you - if you love the sea and water as I do, do this trip. History and beauty all packaged neatly.

END OF MY TRAVELS?

Will I write any more just of travels and travel impressions...and wonderful people? I really don't know. Maybe I feel this stuff more than most. Maybe I'll have the time and energy to do more.

I only hope some of all this has been fun for you to read.

Acknowledgement

First and foremost I want to say thanks to Mary, my wife, who knew how much I wanted to write and how much I needed to travel. I've always been a bit independent in my ways, getting away fishing, playing ball beyond my years, dragging all manner of dog home, and most happily for her, changing jobs far too often. I'd managed to pay most bills but easy I wasn't. My children, Pam and Diane and Steve, too tolerated their father. And even seemed to encourage me from time to time. Thanks, you guys, for being great people.

The satire, and my opinions barely showing through, are dedicated with thanks to my grandchildren Steven, Baird, Dominic, Gabriel and Beth. Especially to Dom who insisted that I dedicate everything to him. Sorry Dom...you must share but thanks for asking. You helped me with one piece, though, I'll tell you about. You all, with your incredibly sharp minds and gifts for clowning, not to mention special skills in the game I love so much, baseball - keep me young.

For her story, I want to say thanks to Gosia, who may think she owes me, but who inspired me to write in two ways - by coming to the States and then proving us both right, and by saying "awesome" when I told her I had some writing ideas. You, Gosia, changed my life as much as I did yours. To you, Ann Ferro, thanks for saying yes.

The last part of this book, the travel vignettes, I dedicate to Diane, who so many times asked me of my life's experience. I could think of no better way to tell her than to couch whatever I did in where I had to be.

Also, for your nice words I'd like to thank my early readers Joan, Arthur, Arthur, Roz and Diane. And Walery especially…and Paul and Ann.

Life is good. Kotilka is now twenty.

The end of an ostrich egg?

Made in the USA
Middletown, DE
17 April 2017